M000100545

Communicate and Motivate

The School Leader's Guide to Effective Communication

Shelly Arneson

Eye on Education
6 Depot Way West, Suite 106
Larchmont, NY 10538
(914) 833-0551
(914) 833-0761 fax
www.eyeoneducation.com

For information about permission to reproduce selections
from this book, write: Eye On Education, Permissions Dept.,
Suite 106, 6 Depot Way West, Larchmont, NY 10538

Library of Congress Cataloging-in-Publication Data

Arneson, Shelly.
Communicate and motivate : the school leader's guide to
effective communication/by Shelly Arneson.
        p.   cm.
Includes bibliographical references.
ISBN 978-1-59667-179-9
1. School administrators—Handbooks, manuals, etc.
2. Communication in education—Handbooks, manuals, etc.
I. Title.

LB2831.8.A76 2011
370.1′4—dc22   2011000925

10 9 8 7 6 5 4 3 2 1

Also Available from EYE ON EDUCATION

Leading School Change:
Nine Strategies to Bring Everybody on Board
Todd Whitaker

Classroom Walkthroughs to Improve Teaching and Learning
Donald Kachur, Judy Stout, and Claudia Edwards

Professional Development: What Works
Sally J. Zepeda

Motivating and Inspiring Teachers: The Educational Leader's
Guide for Building Staff Morale, 2nd Edition
Todd Whitaker, Beth Whitaker, and Dale Lumpa

What Great Principals Do *Differently*:
Fifteen Things That Matter Most
Todd Whitaker

High-Impact Leadership for High-Impact Schools:
The Actions that Matter Most
Pamela Salazar

Principals Who Dare to Care
A. William Place

Get Organized! Time Management for School Leaders
Frank Buck

Applying Servant Leadership in Today's Schools
Mary K Culver

What Do You Say When . . . ?
Best Practice Language for Improving Student Behavior
Hal Holloman and Peggy H. Yates

Rigorous Schools and Classrooms: Leading the Way
Ronald Williamson and Barbara R. Blackburn

Differentiation Is an Expectation:
A School Leader's Guide to Building a Culture of Differentiation
Kimberly K. Hewitt and Daniel J. Weckstein

Dedication

I wish to thank all of the faculty, staff, parents, and students at Edge Elementary School in Niceville, Florida for helping me work on communication skills first-hand as the leader of such an amazing school. I also want to thank my mother and her belief in me when she said her "little fairy will write a book one day." She was my biggest fan. Finally, a huge debt of gratitude goes to my adoring and mutually adored husband, Dave, who has been a faithful editor and honest critic, for assuming the role of biggest fan after Mother's passing.

Biography

Shelly Arneson is a principal at Edge Elementary School and is currently pursuing her doctorate in education. She was previously a teacher then a guidance counselor before becoming a principal six years ago. She lives with her husband Dave and their three Labrador Retrievers in Niceville, Florida. She has presented workshops on leadership and communication at ASCD and enjoys writing fiction as well as educational books. In her free time, Shelly enjoys travelling and reading. Check out her blog at www.principalcommunicates.wordpress.com.

Table of Contents

Preface

When I have presented workshops about principal/teacher communication, participants will make comments such as, "This is such a common sense topic, but it is so important that we hear more about it." I like to conclude the presentation by singing a song called "Legacy" by Nichole Nordeman that challenges each of us to figure out what legacy we wish to leave behind with each encounter we have with others. Because we do . . . leave a legacy, that is. With every conversation we have with teachers and staff members, instructional leaders leave an impression or a legacy. What will they say after their conversations with us? We have the responsibility to ensure that what is said after each exchange is worthy of the role of instructional leader we were hired to be.

Communicate and Motivate is written primarily for principals and other school district leaders, but would also be quite helpful for teacher leaders such as grade level chairpersons, counselors, and instructional coaches. Educational leadership professors would find it beneficial to assign as additional reading in their coursework. Essentially, the book is designed for anyone who is interested in improving communication skills with teachers. The book is written for people who *want* to get better, not necessarily for people who *need* to get better. Why the distinction? We will only gain something if we have the willingness. We have to have the willingness to grow in order to actually grow.

In speaking with other principals in Okaloosa County, Florida and throughout the country, the resounding theme is one of frustration in communicating with teachers. While most principals have good rapport with most of their teachers, many express frustration with the negativity that resonates from a handful of teachers. Comments such as, "The teachers aren't willing to grow or change," "Teachers in my school get so defensive when a parent asks them a simple question," and, "I am so frustrated after talking with my teachers," are just a few, indicating a need for improved communication and relationship building.

Communicate and Motivate contains timeless advice as well as tips from my seventeen years as a teacher and counselor and my six years as a principal. The book also includes anecdotal and motivational real life examples of how to (as well as how not to) communicate with teachers in our schools. After all, if we want to make a change in teachers, what good are our best "instructional leader words of wisdom" if our audience shuts down in the first five minutes because of *how* we said something?

It is time for a more in-depth approach not only to building the relationships with teachers, but also maintaining and keeping those relationships through effective communication techniques.

Outline of Chapter Titles

1. Make Time for Courageous Conversations
It's time to pull the elephant out from underneath the rug and have tough conversations—about student achievement, classroom discipline, and teacher/parent interactions. These conversations, while rarely easy, deserve a proper time and place in which to address the issues we are bringing to light. Knowing when and where to broach these difficult topics is important to the outcome of the conversation.

2. It's Not What You Say, But How You Say It
Principals can tell teachers that they need to work on incorporating more technology into their teaching and have them leave either saying, "My principal doesn't know what she's talking about. I don't care what she says anymore," or, "Wow, my principal has given me some real food for thought today. I need to think carefully about the points she made." The deciding factor is how we, as instructional leaders, present our constructive criticism to the teacher.

3. What You Say Matters, Too, So Choose Your Words Carefully

What's the difference between saying, "You need to work on . . ." versus, "How can I help you improve in . . ."? We teach the students at our school to "stop and think" before they speak or act. We, as principals, should do the same. If we choose our words carefully instead of spewing out every thought and emotion, our words will more likely be "effective and productive."

4. Seek First to Understand

This is where we get ourselves into the most trouble. We must have the willingness to admit that the way the conversation is going is not working and agree to back up and do a little bit of Stephen Covey's "Seek First to Understand . . ." (Covey, 1989) before we can then be understood. Focusing solely on getting our point or agenda across will ultimately lose the teacher in the process.

5. One-on-One Conversations

We need to make the time for talking about important issues—not just in faculty meetings, but in one-on-one conversations with our teachers. They need to hear that we care about them and what they are doing in the classroom and around the school.

6. Avoid Defensiveness

We can almost see a physical wall go up when we tune people out. When our defenses are raised to this level, we can no longer hear. Specific techniques to lower the wall once it's up are discussed. But better yet, let's talk about how to keep it from ever rising in the first place.

7. Let's Not Call the Whole Thing Off . . . Yet

Is the principal/teacher relationship that is struggling because of our ineffective communication worth saving? If it is, we must have the willingness to be the professional. The book and workshops focus on proactive ways we can aid conversations while remaining professional. At the end of the day, however, we as educational leaders must remain professional even if the other person does not.

8. Improving Parent/Teacher Communication From the Inside-Out

How do we want to see teachers communicate with parents? Motivating and surprising role-playing activities created to model examples and non-examples of good communication can be an experiential asset and are explained in depth.

9. When to Use and Avoid Online Communication

The enormous conveniences as well as some dangers of e-mail are discussed in depth in this chapter. Inherent in this form of communication are necessary precautions. This chapter explores the benefits of sending quick, positive notes to teachers via e-mail, but will also give examples of when e-mail communication should *not* be used or should be avoided at the very least. Other online communication tools are also discussed.

10. The Legacy of Effective Communication

What do teachers and parents say about us after they leave our offices? We want it said of us that we "talk the talk" but that we also "walk the walk." Beginning each conversation with this in mind will better enable effective communication. Exercises and challenges on leaving a communication legacy behind are discussed in this chapter.

Points to Ponder

Throughout this book you will be presented with "Points to Ponder," appearing in bubbles at the top or bottom of a page. These "Points" can be used as discussion prompts for students or school leaders in a book study, or reflective pauses for solo readers. However you use the book, these bubbles are meant to give you pause. As the book is intended to help us grow as instructional leaders—and growth requires thought—use these questions and statements to challenge yourself to change and grow in your communication practices.

Introduction

Take a moment to think back on the last conversation you had with one of the teachers at your school. Are you cringing yet? I ask participants (principals, superintendents, and other school leaders) who come to workshops to describe their most recent conversation using popular song titles and lyrics. For example, who relates to "Crazy" by Patsy Cline? What about "You Don't Bring Me Flowers Anymore"? Perhaps you are reminded of "Breaking Up is Hard to Do." "Take This Job and Shove It"? Maybe not quite that extreme. In all sincerity, when I mention these songs and many others, workshop participants may laugh out loud, but they are simultaneously nodding their heads in vigorous agreement. Surprisingly, or maybe not so, "What a Wonderful World" doesn't get as many takers. Why the reaction? It seems that many of us are currently struggling with how to communicate effectively with our teachers (and support staff and parents and maybe even spouses and children, but those will have to wait for another book).

How can communication be so difficult when we do it every day? Since birth, or shortly after, we've been communicating to meet our needs. Surely we should be proficient at it by now. Part of the problem lies in choosing the correct words to say what we really mean, but more often than not, we are faced with the struggle of how to say what we need to say in an effective manner. As a teacher, guidance counselor, and principal, I have seen breakdowns in communication occur less because of *what* we say but more because of *how* we say it (and even when and where we say it, as well).

One of Stephen Covey's "Seven Habits of Highly Effective People" is "Seek first to understand, then to be understood" (Covey, 1989). For most of us, these are mere words to which we

Point to Ponder Try this engaging strategy with teachers at school the day before school starts, perhaps right before an Open House or parent meetings. Ask them "How are you feeling right now about the new school year?" and play a CD filled with clips from songs like "Crazy," "Everybody's Working for the Weekend," "Celebrate," "It's My Party, and I'll Cry if I Want To," etc. You can even put the names of the songs on posterboard or chart tablet paper around the room in which you are meeting and ask teachers to move to the song that they relate to most while you play a montage of the song clips. This is a fun conversation starter. For more creative groups, have them come up with their own titles.

pay lip service. Do we talk *at* people, *to* people, or *with* people? Perhaps we say we are going to communicate, but we have our agenda already prepared and find ourselves unwilling (if not unable) to budge from our mission. Maybe we have gotten into bad habits of multi-tasking while trying to hold a conversation with our teachers. Just as significant, we may have important words of wisdom to share with our teachers about communication, but we are not "walking the walk" or actively modeling these skills ourselves. Teachers see the words as "empty" if they don't see us walking the walk ourselves. Whatever the reason, you probably didn't pick up this book if the lyrics you chose to represent your most recent principal/teacher conversations were more along the lines of "Everything is Beautiful." My fervent hope is that you will find the chapters in this book useful, enlightening, and yes, perhaps at times humorous, since laughing at ourselves is one great way to relieve stress as school leaders.

1

Make Time for Courageous Conversations

First Things First—Be Seen as the School Leader

Before I was hired to be the principal at an elementary school in northwest Florida, I was the guidance counselor at the same school for several years. The principal who preceded me gave me some sound advice before he retired. "When you come back from lunch or after you've done a few classroom walkthroughs," he said, "walk back to the office via a different route." His point was that we need to get out of our routines and make sure we, as the leaders in our school, see everything and are seen everywhere. Leaders need to be visible. "When the cat is away, the mice will play" may sound like a silly analogy. The majority of good teachers don't need the principal in their classrooms on a daily basis. They are self-starters, motivated instructors, who are going to do good, solid work regardless of who is in the building or in their classroom. But the necessity of having the presence of a principal in a school is most obvious when that leader is absent.

In an effort to cut costs, two local elementary schools were forced to share a principal. The parents, teachers, and students felt the absence. Discipline issues increased, test scores suffered, and faculty morale plummeted. Employees at one school even admitted that they had developed a code that signaled others when the principal was on their campus. The principal was well-trained, great at motivating teachers, and desperately wanted to make the school-sharing a success. However, it soon became obvious that consistent presence is a necessity. Educational leaders are crucial to a school's well-being in many ways and the best way we can be a part of the culture is to observe and be observed.

But let's be honest. Raise your hand if you have ever walked down the hallway and made a sharp left or right in a door or out a door when you suddenly saw that teacher who seemed to be the first in line at least once a week to come to your office with a concern or complaint. The point is that we have all experienced the desire to hide from what we need to do, at one time or another. Eleanor Roosevelt (1960) said, "You must do the thing you cannot do" (p. 30). This quote is a challenge to those of us who lead our schools. It is time to face the music of courageous conversations with all the teachers with whom we work at school, whether we want to or not. Rosanne Cash (1993) said, "The key to change is to let go of fear." What are we doing today to let go of the fear that keeps us from changing?

But when and where shall we begin? Perhaps we should first start with when and where we should *not* hold these conversations. Just as we caution teachers to avoid having difficult talks with parents or co-workers in the hallways or in other public areas, we should make the commitment to avoid the same. What is the problem with these particularly public encounters? Not only is the tension likely to be exacerbated for the participants, but the air around the school can quickly become "poisoned" for the audience who unwittingly or purposefully overhears such talk. People feel uncomfortable hearing negative talk. It is, however, like the proverbial train wreck. "I can't bear to see the horrific devastation," we say as we peek through our fingers at the wreckage. But what do we do next? Go share the terrible details with 10 of our closest friends.

Difficult conversations are better off reserved for a private location behind closed doors. Parents and teachers joke that I have an always-open-door policy because I really do hate to shut it for fear that someone might have a concern that goes unasked or unsaid. Do you recall the scene in *Dangerous Minds* when Louanne Johnson, the spunky teacher played by Michelle Pfeiffer, finds out that the principal sent away one of her high school students who was trying to report someone trying to kill him because the student had walked in the office without knocking on the door? The victim ended up being killed that

Point to Ponder Are you accessible? How do you make time for conversations with students? Parents? Faculty?

morning. When the counselor encourages Louanne to talk to her students about what had happened, she asks, "What should I tell them? If they don't want to die, remember to knock?" School leaders, in my opinion, should be accessible to everyone.

The time the door should get shut, however, is during serious conversations with teachers or parents that don't need to be witnessed by the rest of the school. The principal's office should be a safe haven to share concerns, for students, parents, teachers, and the principal alike. Don't think for an instant that people won't hear those conversations you try to keep at a whisper level when your door remains open. The front-office/ front-lines secretary at our school (let's just call her the magical, Genie-in-a-bottle, tamer of wild beasts, wonder woman, for lack of a better term) and I have often remarked that if you talk about people, they will appear. I learned this lesson the hard way when new to counseling, and I must admit I still have to be reminded of the same lesson: shut your door if you need to have a private conversation because people do listen and they do hear, especially when we would rather they not. It is simply a life lesson we all must learn and heed, lest we lose credibility with our stakeholders. That reputation takes a good while to be built up, but only a split-second to be knocked down.

Finding Time

Another concern is finding the time to talk. Making the time for courageous conversations may sound like a great endeavor, but it is often a difficult task. A few years ago, I interviewed and subsequently hired a teacher from a neighboring school. While I could tell immediately that she was an excellent teacher, she began a habit of sending me e-mails, asking if she could make appointments with me on a regular basis. When we met at the designated time, she asked me questions that easily and quickly could have been answered in passing or via e-mail. When I questioned her about this issue, she confided to me that at her previous school, the principal seemed to never have time for her concerns. She had learned that the only way to get face time was to make an appointment. She had an excellent point. We work in a world of rapidly moving days that seem to fly by right in front of our very eyes. How many times do you find yourself looking at the clock only to realize that you have ten minutes until dismissal and you never got a chance to take a break or to even eat lunch? If we are not careful, we will fritter away our days without making the time for teachers—the very people who are most crucial to the success of our schools. As the school year draws to a close, we should not regret the time we spent at school and we won't if the bulk of the time was spent with people. The paperwork is always going to be there and it's probably going to be easier to do when our stakeholders are gone for the day, anyway. Therefore, even when the "frequent flyer award winners" come to our door to justify their reaction to a parent or to rationalize why they didn't turn in their lesson plans the past weekend, we simply must make the time.

Suggestions for how principals can make time:

◆ Come before school a half hour early. Have you ever noticed how much work you can get finished when nobody else is around?
◆ Stay a bit later to catch up on e-mails, phone calls, etc.
◆ Delegate, delegate, delegate.

In other words, make sure your time at school is worthy of what you were hired to do and be, which is the instructional leading of the school. If we can take care of some of the minutia outside of the time when teachers and students are there, our time while they are there can be devoted to better student, staff, and parent interactions.

Sometimes we honestly don't have the time at that moment. When this happens, we owe it to everyone to be upfront. Every year at the beginning of the school year, I make sure to tell parents and teachers one important note: "If you come to see me,"

I advise them, "I might not be in my office. My most important role is to be out and about in the school with your children and your children's teachers. Even if I am in my office, I will tell you right away if I have to leave shortly to attend another meeting, so we can make an appointment to talk. *Listening to your concern is too important to talk about it when we don't have time.*"

We must ask parents to give the same respect for time to teachers. The parent who wants to talk to the teacher while the teacher is getting class started is disrupting the very important routine process a la Harry Wong (2009). Telling a parent that their concern is so important that it deserves more time than you can give at the moment makes all the difference in the world. Furthermore, if we have spent the time building relationships with people as Stephen Covey (1989) says is so crucial for that emotional bank account between any two people, it won't be so devastating to make a withdrawal here and there when you have to say, "Can we talk at 1:00 this afternoon? I have to rush out to do an observation now." Building the emotional bank accounts with our stakeholders is time consuming, but it is worth it. Relationships matter.

Making time to talk is a sign of respect for our teachers and our profession, one we as educational leaders cannot afford to forsake.

How to Start Courageous Conversations

Now that you have the teacher locked in your office (just kidding; you should never lock teachers in your office), it is time to begin. Stephen Covey's first habit of effective people is to be proactive (1989). This is an especially important step for educational leaders. A good start is the best indication of how well a conversation will turn out. But how shall we make that good start? Having made the mistake myself of beginning conversations without this forethought or pre-planning, I am sad to report that lack of preparedness shines through like a beacon in the night.

After hearing an extremely talented and strong teacher make a comment that sounded quite negative (something about "sometimes good is good enough—we don't have to be great teachers") in front of a group of other teacher leaders, I wanted to find out what was going on. But instead of starting the conversation by asking a *question*, I made the mistake of making a *statement* instead. "I was surprised and even a little disappointed," I began, "to hear you say that you thought 'good was good enough.'" Even though I immediately noticed her visibly bristle, I felt I had a point I needed to make. Therein lies the rub with so many conversations that go awry. Sometimes, we are so bent on pressing our own agenda, we forget that in order for the message to be received, the other party must be in receiving mode. Anyway, what difference does it make if you are right when the other person doesn't hear you? Ensuring the receiver is in the mode to receive is a vital part of the preparation.

In the previous instance, a question might have been a much more appropriate beginning for the conversation. Can you think of one I could have used? Naturally, it's always easier when you are the not the one on the hot seat. That's the point of the proactive, pre-planning. We think ahead to how we might react if someone started a talk with us the way we are proposing to start the pending conversation.

Clearly, hindsight truly is 20/20 and I could later more easily see that I might have started with a question like, "How did you feel the meeting went yesterday?" She might have even had a general sense that what she had said had not been well-received by other parties, and beginning with a question might have been just the opening she needed to admit her ill-chosen words. As it was, I had to respect that she had said what she said out of a bit of frustration in trying to do it all, and she was able to ultimately see how I could have been a bit frustrated with her comment.

Point to Ponder Think of the last time you *told* a teacher something they "needed to hear." Can you think of a question you could have *asked* instead that might have opened the door to better communication? How might it have changed the outcome of the conversation?

Perhaps it is helpful to try to frame our concerns as open-ended questions in situations like this. For example, "How did you think the meeting went?" or "How do you feel your comment was received by the group?"

Planning for difficult conversations is a step not to be missed. How, when, and where you plan is a matter of taste. I often find myself pre-planning for what I anticipate will be a difficult conversation by using my husband to role-play. We have even found these role-plays beneficial in helping us with our own communication as well. After all, how can we role-play an effective communication and then turn around and be ugly to one another? As a side-note, what we practice in our professional lives bleeds over into our personal lives and vice-versa.

Obviously, you can't plan for all the variables that may occur. Keep in mind we are dealing with human beings. Human beings are fallible, unpredictable, and sometimes even just a little "nuts." However, being proactive can eliminate many communication mistakes. In my experience, no conversation ever ended worse after preparing for it. On the contrary, most end up being much more productive. The following are simple tips to prepare for the difficult conversation.

- ◆ *Think of your opening line.* "I'm so glad you came in to talk about this," works so much more effectively than, "You know why I asked you to come see me, don't you?"
- ◆ *Practice those tough sentences you have to say.* Clearly, it is better to state, "I will look forward to hearing how your talk with that parent goes by the end of this

Point to Ponder What good do you put in before a tough conference with a teacher or parent? My suggestion is to play some uplifting music, get in a calm state of mind, find a great quote you want to use, and think ahead to how you envision the conversation ending (and "quickly" doesn't suffice for how you wish it to end).

week," than it is to say, "You're going to take care of that, right, so I don't get another phone call?"

◆ *Put good thoughts in and you'll likely experience better success.* Hopefully, it doesn't sound trite to be reminded that if we want good to come out, we need to put good in.

◆ *Establish ground rules.* Ground rules set the tone for the upcoming meeting. They might be as simple as, "Listen to each other without interrupting," and, "Keep an open mind even if you think you might disagree," but they allow all participants to be on a level playing field.

Pull the Elephant Out From Underneath the Rug

A few years back, a principal friend of mine had a problem with the school's guidance counselor. The counselor was reportedly talking behind the principal's back. This principal found herself frustrated with the behind-the-back chatter she was hearing. Unfortunately, instead of making time to confront the counselor, she began doing the same thing—she found herself "leaking" to teachers that the counselor couldn't be trusted. We must go to the source immediately and get things out on the table. Behind-the-scenes assumptions will only further the misunderstandings. Direct communication can often be difficult, particularly if there are some inherent differences in opinion between two people, but the longer the delay in initiating the communication, the more volatile the environment becomes. In the previous instance, the principal and guidance counselor never

Point to Ponder Think of a misunderstanding you have experienced. What could have prevented it? Did it ever get resolved? Do you still maintain hurt feelings over it? Do you avoid the person with whom you had the disagreement or misunderstanding?

did resolve their problems and the guidance counselor simply left to take another position.

This scenario probably happens more often than we care to admit—when we can't resolve our differences, sometimes we just walk away. What remains, however, are the hurt feelings and lingering blame that never really heal because we didn't talk about them.

Instead, we need to take some time to face our fears and talk about the elephant that sits under the rug. You know he's there, everyone knows he's there, but not one person says, "Hey elephant. Come out from underneath that rug!"

I recently sat in on a parent/teacher conference in which the teacher was trying to let the parents know how much their son was struggling to focus in the classroom. Donna, the teacher, was doing a very nice job until the parents began visibly bristling. Donna didn't seem to notice. Oblivious, the teacher continued with her assessment of how the student was doing in reading, and the parents became more silent and withdrawn. Donna didn't notice. I noticed. It is infinitely easier to be objective and notice things like this when you aren't in the heat of the battle. Before the conference became totally unproductive, I called a time-out and pulled the elephant out. "Mr. and Mrs. Henderson," I began, "I cannot help but notice that you are looking really frustrated. We need your help with this situation, so I am asking you to not shut down. What's going on?" From out of nowhere, the dad looked at me and said, "I'm not putting him on medication." *What*? Nothing had ever been said about medication, but they had the *perception* that the teacher's evaluation of the student's performance in class was going to lead to a discussion of his need for medicine. The next statement seemed to help clarify our purpose a bit. "Our primary purpose in meeting today," I reminded everyone, "is to brainstorm in order to further help your child. We need to get past any feelings that anyone is going to finger-point so we can get on with the business of helping your child succeed. Can we focus on solutions?" Interestingly, the conference continued without a hitch.

In another instance, an issue of student achievement needed to be addressed with a third-grade teacher. Perhaps because she was very close to retirement, she seemed to be resisting differentiation in reading for her students and felt whole-group reading instruction worked best. After efforts by the Literacy Coach and strong teacher leaders on her grade level had failed to alter her views, it was time to step in. Two parents indicated that, while they felt she was a nice, fair teacher in many respects, their children weren't getting the same differentiated experiences as they did in other classes. During her mid-year review, she and the principal sat down and looked at some reading assessment data. They talked about the need to teach reading in small groups and she seemed to agree and acknowledge. One week later, in a classroom walkthrough, the principal noticed that her reading table was cluttered with books and papers. As much as she hated to be confrontational, the principal had to ask her, "How are you teaching small group reading when you don't seem to have room at your reading table to sit with a group?" She realized she needed to start by clearing off the table and making room for new learning. The school then arranged for the Literacy Coach to come in and model different ways of setting up and running reading groups to help ease her transition.

How, when, and where we begin our courageous conversations can make all the difference in the world between effective and ineffective communication.

2

It's Not What You Say, But How You Say It

Several teachers from a local elementary school were sharing their feelings with me about the relationship with their principal. "I understand," one of them said, "that my principal wants to see my lesson plans each week, but what I don't get is why he has to use a red marker to 'grade' them." Two others chimed in and openly complained, "He is treating us like children!" The teachers felt that the grading of lesson plans was not only demeaning but also had harmed their relationship with him. Not only did they resent it, they didn't feel safe anymore. I suspect that the principal's intention was to highlight areas of their lesson plans he had questions about and to ask those probing questions we have been taught to ask, not to red mark the plans for the sake of embarrassment or demeaning the teachers. The problem in so many instances such as this is that the intent and the received perception are not in sync. We think we are saying something in a curious tone and it comes off as accusatory.

What and how something is said can have lasting effects on those around us. Misunderstandings occur every minute of every day based on what or how we say something. Either our words are convoluted, the message is masked in emotion, or the innuendos of sarcasm or teasing are lost on the receiver. Whatever the case, the sender's message did not make it to the receiver's ears or brain correctly.

My mother told a story years ago about a time when she and my father were asked to come over to the house of some friends one evening "for a pizza pie." They got a babysitter for my sister and me, starved themselves all day in preparation for a huge pizza dinner, and drove to the get-together at 7:30 that evening. As the story goes, my mother and father waited patiently for about an hour, talking, laughing, but decidedly getting hungrier by the minute, until the lady of the house finally went into the kitchen and walked back into the living room bearing nothing other than slivers of lemon pie. "A piece of pie" was what my parents had unwittingly and unknowingly agreed to, and after a few more minutes of pleasantries (and probably licking every crumb of that pie off the plate), they bid their adieus and left for an all-night diner to scarf down on *real* food.

A simple misunderstanding because of the actual words used is one thing. But misunderstandings between principals and teachers happen every day, due, in part, to the frantic, breakneck speed at which we sometimes to have to operate. Have you ever noticed that you are more likely to lose things (car keys, wallet, watch, important bills to pay, etc.) when you are in a huge hurry? This isn't just me, is it? It is likely that the reason for this strange phenomenon has less to do with Murphy's Law and more to do more with the hectic speed at which we are trying to accomplish 4,000,000 things all at once?

At school, principals and teachers seem to be constantly operating at this pace and, therefore, communication is more likely to cause confusion. Simple things like, "I'd like to see your lesson plans for this week," demands the question, "Which week? This current one or this *next* one?" Who is wrong and who is right? And the bigger question is: What difference does it make if communication was skewed?

Emotions play a huge role in the way we communicate and the way we respond to communication. I am currently doing research on how the relationships principals have with teachers at school play a part in how well messages are conveyed between the two parties. My hypothesis (which is not too shocking or earth-shattering) is that the better the relationship, the less cause for misunderstanding or misinterpretation. In the previous example regarding the teachers and the lesson plan, it is worthy to note that one of the teachers who has worked for that principal for a very long time, including time working alongside him before she began to work for him, indicated that she just laughed off the red marked lesson plans. With a wave of her hand, she said, "Oh he doesn't mean anything by that." Is the difference between how the other teachers perceive his lesson plan grading and her perception because of their history? If

Point to Ponder What are some examples of miscommunication or misunderstandings that have occurred in your school and how could you avoid the same misunderstandings in the future?

relationships matter so much, perhaps we all need to take more time in developing them.

No matter the relationship between principals and teachers, though, the fact remains that our words and how we convey them have an effect (either intended or unintended) on other people.

How people react to what we say or how we say it depends a good deal on our sincerity. Trust has a way of levelizing difficult conversations. Much research has been conducted on the trust between teachers and principals. When I was first hired to be a principal in our county, the superintendent at the time called me to congratulate me on the new job. He said he wanted to make sure I understood one thing: "I am always in your shopping cart." We had a great relationship already and I was not offended by this comment. I understood that he meant we, as school leaders, should be cautious about when, where, and how we talk to people in public about what is going on at our school. However, when I shared his comment with someone else, the person was shocked that I wasn't hurt by it. The comment sounded rude and demeaning to the person. I didn't see it as such. Why? I believe the defining reason is that the superintendent and I had established an emotional bank account.

We have to be so careful of how we word things. Sarcasm is a cutting or biting remark or expression that is intended to dig or to make a point. One of the many problems with sarcasm is that not everyone possesses the same perception and, therefore, not all can really get it or understand when sarcasm is being used. Take, for example, the teacher who says to her entire class, "Joey has been disrupting your learning today, hasn't he? Well, if I were you, I would just go straight home and tell your parents that you were not able to do any of your work today because of Joey's classroom behavior." Yikes! But how different is that from the school leader who says to her faculty, "If you think my job is easy, I invite any one of you to come stand up here and take over for me. Anyone interested? Of course not. Nobody wants to do what I do." Double yikes! Sarcasm is a deadly foe when dealing with employees, especially ones with whom a principal has not yet established a relationship. How disconcerting to be a teacher and have a supervisor make a comment that prompts the question, "Is he joking with me or not?" A leader's best tools are honesty and a forthright demeanor, and sarcasm negates a good deal of both of those. Teachers need principals to be open and honest with them about their progress, evaluations, classroom management, parent concerns, and so much more. If a principal has to give constructive feedback to a teacher, that teacher deserves the right to know that the principal is being upfront with him or her. I once had a middle school principal say to our faculty, "I enjoy the relationships I have built with you all so much, but I have to be so careful. How can I joke around with you guys too much and then have to put on my bad guy hat to tell you that I have a problem with the way you are doing something?" Good point. Plus, and perhaps most importantly, a principal who uses sarcasm with a teacher is simply role modeling for the teacher how to treat the students in the classroom. Scary thought, isn't it?

Another big drain on our ability to exude sincerity is how well we compliment our teachers. The old saying goes, "We should give three compliments for every negative comment." I wholeheartedly agree. We all need to hear what we are doing well from our supervisors. There is so much implied in this necessity, however. First of all, in order to compliment the teachers on a job well done, we first have to name what that job is. In Classroom Walkthroughs, we are looking at specific teaching and learning behaviors. Whatever the focus in your individual state, district, or even school, the teachers need to know exactly what is being looked for. Is it Marzano's highly effective strategies? These are great choices. Is it classroom management a la Harry Wong? More great choices. Is it good sound practices that give feedback to the student and allow the teacher to teach as in Doug Lemov's book *Teach Like a Champion*? Another great source for look-fors. But whatever it is, we have to name it.

Point to Ponder Has anyone ever used sarcasm on you when you weren't sure if they were joking or not? How did you respond?

Have you ever used it on an employee? What was the effect?

The same holds true for parent conferencing, writing individual professional development goals, or participating in a teacher book study. If a principal expects teachers to do something, that something needs to be named. I've heard it said many times, "What you inspect, you expect." I hope the teachers in our schools know that what we are looking for when we walk through their classrooms are the very behaviors that we expect to see each and every day. And, by the way, I need to role-model those teaching behaviors myself. During professional development and workshops for teachers, I will often point out when I have caught myself asking multiple questions before getting a response or not giving enough wait-time for people to ponder their responses before calling on someone.

Second of all, the teachers actually have to be caught doing a good job with whatever teaching behaviors have been named. In other words, the principal must be a presence in the building. I heard a teacher once describe his principal's school routine as "sit, swivel, and visit." The principal was always available in the office to take a minute for a teacher who had a question. If the phone rang, he would swivel to the phone. If the e-mail chimed "You've got mail," he would swivel to answer the call of Microsoft Outlook. But the principal had no idea, except via hearsay, what the teachers were doing in the classroom. How can a principal compliment someone on a job well done if he never sees the job being well done? So, the desired teaching behaviors must be viewed or claimed.

Finally, the desired teaching behaviors must be recognized. You know your faculty. Do they want to be recognized out loud in a faculty meeting? Do they want to read about who did what in a weekly newsletter? (I call mine the Friday Focus and I always try to include some little tidbit about how a teacher was using her transition times to encourage higher-order thinking in math, etc.). Or, perhaps they just want to be told in person as you walk past them in the hallway ("Hey, I loved watching the lesson narrative writing tips. I hope you don't mind me sharing those with others"). I like notepads (I buy tons of different kinds) because I like the permanence that the writing gives. Find your style. Regardless of the method, the desired teaching behaviors need to be "famed" or brought to light. My three Labrador Retrievers learned as puppies that we reward certain behaviors. They lay down on the floor in the kitchen before we put down their dog bowls at feeding time. Human nature is not so different, is it? Who among us hasn't been complimented for some talent, skill, favor, or good work only to find ourselves thinking about doing it just as well, if not better, the next time that person is watching? At a principal's meeting, if our superintendent compliments someone for bringing in an interesting article for us to peruse, five more people will be doing the same thing at the next meeting.

At school, as I walk through classrooms, I like to notice good writing among the students, particularly from those I know have struggled with this skill in the past. Lo and behold, the very next time I walk into that classroom, I find that same student almost showing off his or her writing to me. Even if they aren't allowed to call out when I walk through the room, I've watched a little boy poised in his desk so that his paper is open for my viewing as I pass by. If you think about it, educators are not any different. We want for our good work to be noticed.

Compliments are important to all of us. If we should compliment three times for every constructive criticism we give, it may be because if we don't, that criticism might not be taken as well. So, in my evaluations, classroom walkthroughs, or general conversations with my teachers, I should outweigh my suggestions with comments about the good things I see going on in the classroom, lesson plans, or assessments, lest my feedback fall on deaf ears.

One caveat is that the praise must be completely sincere in order to be effective. Long gone are the days when "Good job" and "Way to go" were enough for kids, teachers, or anyone else for that matter. Many teachers have used this general praise in

Point to Ponder Which one of these do you find easiest to do? Which one do you need to work on?

their classrooms (if I had a nickel for every time I told my students "Good job" the first year I taught, I would be able to retire early) only to find other students looking around, wondering, "Who did something good?" "What did they do that was good?" and, "How can I get complimented on that?" Teachers can begin to feel the same way if principals don't use praise effectively. If we simply write in a Friday newsletter, "Good job on lesson plans," I will likely get at least three questions from various teachers: "Were mine okay?" "Was there anything wrong with my lesson plans?" and, "What should I do differently to make mine better?"

The praise should also be very specific. Just as students crave and need feedback that is specific to their skill set, so do teachers. If I visit a classroom then say as I walk out, "Great lesson!" that is one thing. If, however, I write the teacher a note saying, "Wow! I was impressed that your students could tell you (and me) that the point of today's lesson was to find inferences in the story. Your higher-order questions made the students really think, especially the one, 'How would the character from last week's story have handled the same dilemma as the one from today?'" This type of specific feedback will let the teacher know which high-yield strategies you expect to see them continue to use in future lessons.

In review, if we want to increase effective teaching behaviors, we have to name them, claim them, and "fame" them.

1. Name the behavior.
2. Claim the behavior.
3. Fame the behavior.

3

What You Say Matters, Too, So Choose Your Words Carefully

With drug education and anti-bullying programs, "I-Messages" are taught to students across the country. In Drug Education lessons, students are taught the verbage so they will use that verbage if they are faced with negative peer pressure. I-messages keep us from pointing the finger at others and allow us to take responsibility for the way we are feeling. There is obviously a time and place to use different language than this. Students who have repeatedly been bullied should not have to sit in a room and tell the bully how they feel. But most of us working in school systems would do well to use I-messages more frequently than we currently do.

In dealing with bullying situations as a guidance counselor and now as a principal, I have found one of the things lacking in our vocabulary is the ability to tell someone effectively how we feel about how their behavior impacts us. So, while we vehemently say we have zero tolerance for any bullying in school or on the bus or over the internet, we must also be vigilant about addressing the ability for students to speak up if and when it does happen to them.

There is a time and place for making I-messages, but more often than not, communication with our employees is likely a good time to do so and to model the same for them. "I feel concerned when I continue to see students from your class crying about the way they perceive you yelling at them," might work a bit better than, "You keep getting complaints from kids in your class about all of your yelling." We have all seen teachers who, out of frustration, snap at the students, "You need to sit down and get quiet," but we also see those great classroom managers who say, "I really like the way 100% of the students on the south side of the room are prepared for the lesson and ready to go!"

Anyone who manages employees deals with the same issues of "how to" communicate. We have to make a paradigm shift if we want to tackle new ways of communicating with employees. My husband, who manages a group of people on an Air Force base, also shares stories of successes and failures. As a systems engineer, his logical nature is a good match for my emotional counselor side. Just the other day, he came home announcing that he needed to confront one of his employees at work who had written an e-mail that reeked of insubordination. My husband repeatedly used the words, "I need to warn him he better watch out." Every time I heard that phrase, I suspect I visibly winced because shortly after, he stopped and asked, "Okay, what? What am I doing wrong?" I thought about it for a minute then said, "I think the problem is that what you need to tell him is right. I'm afraid the way you plan on telling him will keep him from hearing the message you need him to hear. Then what?" He changed his wording and scheduled a time to talk to the employee.

Similarly, one of the grade level chairs came in my office one day, shut my door behind her (a sure sign something exciting is about to happen), and proceeded to break down crying as steam poured out of her ears. "Would you like to sit down?" I asked her. Her only reply was to begin pacing back and forth in front of my desk. "I want to resign as grade-level chair and I want to teach another grade level next year," she said calmly (just kidding—you know she didn't say this calmly). I have learned a couple of things in my years as a counselor and principal. Sometimes when people begin to vent, it is wise to not begin talking right away, perhaps not even to respond at all. I just listened as she continued. "My teammates, if you can call them that, don't respect anything I have to say, they never listen, and they always talk over me." After she had lost some of her steam, I was able to ask some of those clarifying questions, "So, what is most frustrating for you?" "How do you know they don't respect you?" and also to tell her good-naturedly that I don't take resignations from grade level chair positions while the person is in a fit of anger. While I could only say this when I have a good relationship with the teacher, I really believe in this process. In my opinion, nobody should ever be allowed to quit anything when they are in the heat of anger. If, after the initial anger passes, the person still feels that resigning from a particular role or position is in their best interests, then it makes sense to talk more seriously about it. However, so many of our mistakes are made when we are in a fit of rage, but after the anger passes, we are left with the consequences of those bad decisions. We encourage students to stop and think, so we should likely do the same before making any major decisions or choices.

When we finally landed on the real issue she had had, she felt that her teammates had questioned her judgment and she felt unloved, unworthy, and targeted. Wow, sounds like how we often feel as administrators, doesn't it? She continued by stating that she was going to go in and tell them, "I can't believe you think that I monopolize the meetings. That makes me mad that you would think that of me." I asked her if she could envision what might happen if she said those words to her grade level. She said, "They'd probably deny saying I monopolize the meetings." "Hmmm . . . then I wonder if a question might be better," I suggested. Before she thought about it, she said, "So I should ask them *why* they think that?" "What do you think they might say if you ask that?" I questioned. "They'd probably still deny saying it . . ." she thought. "So, back up a step." She practiced and rehearsed until she finally decided upon the following: "I know that my role is to be the Grade Level Chair, but I wonder if sometimes I come across as monopolizing the meetings. I want complete honesty. Do you sometimes feel that way?" What a difference a change in wording makes.

Simply beginning with the end in mind can help communication not turn into a nightmare. Altering a few words here and there can make all the difference in the way a conversation turns out.

Many leaders think that it is our job to be direct and honest. I agree. However, if the message you are intending to share— the message that is so important you have made a PowerPoint presentation out of it and rehearsed your whole speech—is lost on your audience because it offends people, then what good was all that effort in the first place? Thumper tried desperately to tell Bambi he was a clumsy oaf, but there was no nice way

Point to Ponder What is that thing that you, as a leader, feel you cannot do? It is worth taking a few moments to identify that which gives us pause, name it, identify it, claim it, and then talk about it.

to say it, so Thumper's mom finally told him "If you can't say something nice, don't say anything at all."

Principals often need to talk to teachers about tough situations. What are your most difficult conversations to have with teachers? About student achievement? What about when parents are complaining about the teacher? Are the most difficult talks the ones about the teacher's evaluation? Each principal leader likely has teachers who are easier than others to talk with, but we all have those who give us pause when they step into the threshold of our office.

Confrontation is not fun, but confrontation must occur sometimes if we are going to do the job we were hired to do. Randy Pausch, in *The Last Lecture* (2008), said, "When there's an elephant in the room, introduce it" (p. 16). It may not be fun, but it is a necessary evil. While working with a group of teachers, if you notice one with arms crossed, shaking her head and sulking, it would be irresponsible to not say something. Calling attention may clear some much needed poison from the air. Eleanor Roosevelt said, "We must do the thing that we cannot do."

Entire twelve-step programs have been based on the premise that the first step in solving a problem is admitting there is a problem. No other work on the addiction or problem can even be half-heartedly attempted until there is an admission that there is, indeed, a problem. If we walk around continually hiding from the people or the issues that give us the most trouble, we will never give ourselves or the people around us the chance to change and grow.

I'm not proud to tell this secret, but I have skirted past teachers, staff, parents, and even kids at the grocery store or at the mall because I did not want to talk to them. What happens, though, is after I have done such a thing, I am not proud of myself and I wind up questioning what I was really trying to avoid in the first place. Sometimes, what I was thinking I wanted to avoid was not an issue in the first place. Case in point: recently, we began taking zoning waivers in order to increase the numbers of students in our school. Several parents from a neighboring school had come to visit and I took some time to show them around the school, touring classrooms, showing off the lunchroom and Media Center and Computer Lab. The families really seemed impressed, ending the tour by telling me they planned on coming to our school the next year. About three weeks later, my secretary got an e-mail from the neighboring school, notifying us that the two families who had toured had decided to remain at their home school. While this was their prerogative, we were certainly curious. I debated for two days about whether or not to try to find out what had changed their minds. Was it the age of our school? Our beautiful, nostalgic school happens to be the oldest building in the county, so I thought perhaps this might be the issue. Maybe it was the fact that we don't offer a formal art program. With all the budget cuts, teachers have had to tackle the job of finding their own art teachers or volunteers. I even wondered at one point if, perhaps, they didn't like me, personally, or maybe I had said something wrong. Finally, enough was enough. I told myself that if I was going to put my communication money where my communication mouth is, I better practice what I preach. I called one of the moms (dare I mention I wanted to make this phone call less than I wanted to have an emergency root canal?) and said I was just doing a follow-up phone call to tell her we had received the e-mail stating that the children would remain at their zoned school. I pressed forward, pausing only slightly to take a short breath when I told her I wanted to see what made the decision for her and if there was anything we could have done that would have convinced her to enroll her kids at our school. Take a guess what her answer was. She thanked me so much for calling then said, " . . . because there must be some misunderstanding. My kids *will* be attending your school. We loved our visit and we still want a zoning waiver." Apparently, the secretary at that neighboring school had gotten some incorrect information and repeated that misunderstanding to our secretary. The point is, we have to be courageous enough to say what we think we

Point to Ponder Can you think of a time when tackling a problem head-on was rewarded with a good outcome? Has it ever backfired?

cannot say, and many times we will be pleasantly surprised at the outcome.

Teachers of behavioral-disordered children learn early on that what they say to their students matters a great deal. The wording and phrasing of sentences could make the difference between compliance and a complete meltdown. Consider the difference between saying, "You better not waste any more time or you won't be going to recess at all today," and, "I want to see how quickly you can get your name on your paper and get started with your writing so you will be ready to go when we head out to recess in 25 minutes." Semantics? Maybe, but choosing our words takes only a few seconds and makes all the difference in the world. It is the same with our teachers. When a teacher pops his head in your office to ask if you are busy, what is your response? "Are you nuts? Of course I'm busy! I'm always busy!" or do you say something more jovial like, "Never too busy for you, Mr. Palmer. What's up?" Relationships are built, maintained, or injured with every conversation or encounter we have with the teachers in our school. Think about that for a minute. Do you believe it? If teachers are watching what we do and listening to what we say all the time (and they are) then it stands to reason that we are role-modeling for them every time we open our mouths. If they come to us to talk, vent, ask for advice, or any other reason, our reaction matters. Not just the reaction we give when we are in a good mood. Not just the reaction on a Friday afternoon when we are about to leave for the weekend. Every reaction matters. Pretty strong words, but it is the truth.

So what do we say if we honestly don't have the time to talk? Honesty is, by far, the best policy, but we should be cautious about how we convey our honesty. If I am headed out to do an observation on a teacher that starts in four minutes, and another teacher walks up to me while I'm walking out of my

Point to Ponder How do you let teachers know you want to hear what they have to say, even when you are in a hurry to go somewhere else?

office, I might say, "I'm on my way to an observation. Do you want to walk with me or do you want to make an appointment to talk a little bit later?" We should convey the message that we don't have much time, but still want to hear what the teacher has to say as soon as possible, or the teacher might begin to take their problems elsewhere.

4

Seek First to Understand

"If I am so busy waiting to have my say, I won't hear what you have to say."

—Shelly Arneson

Stephen Covey (1989) wrote a book about seven habits which, if used correctly, will increase our effectiveness in dealing with other people. Likely one of the most difficult ones to adhere to is "Seek first to understand, then to be understood." This past year, our elementary school began adopting these seven habits in an effort to become more focused on leadership in our school. We had a movie theater theme last year in which we focused on "Now Showing: Leadership." Our current theme is "Growing Leaders . . . one at a time." As we exposed the children to these habits, we also learned ourselves. When I taught a lesson on "Seek first . . ." I had the students break down the whole phrase, one word at a time. Another definition for "seek" is to "try to find." Several students made the connection to setting a goal. You haven't necessarily achieved it yet, but you are committed to trying. Personally, I believe that this commitment to trying is what separates a good idea from one that is put into action. The next word in the habit is "first." That means that before I do anything else, I will do this thing—seek. "To understand" comes next—wow, that is a loaded one. What do we really mean when we say, "I understand"? Do we use that interchangeably with "I hear you"? What are the most difficult things to say you understand? Do you understand when a teacher is going to leave your school in the middle of the semester and you have to buy a long-term substitute position? Do you understand when a teacher says she needs to go to a dental appointment during the third faculty meeting in one month? Do you really understand when a teacher says she is going to file a workman's compensation claim because she climbed up on a chair to dust her television set and fell off and sprained her ankle? I suspect we all have times when we say, "I understand," when we aren't totally positive if we really do. As a former guidance counselor, I taught the concepts of active listening to the children in elementary and middle school, but I myself needed that training as much as I gave it. Believe it or not, the next word "then" is perhaps the most important word. Then implies that I will do it, it's just a matter of time. "I will ride the rollercoaster, then I will throw up." Almost a cause and effect scenario. Who here among us has not said such words to our own children or students? "You may clean your room, then you can play outside." "Be sure you finish your journal entry, then you will be able to play at recess." Listen, and *then* you will be able to be understood. I like it. Somehow the part about being understood is not as difficult for most of us. We make sure that we are understood.

But what does it really mean to be understood? We have all seen the communication flow chart that shows a sender and a receiver. The sender sends a message, but there *is* no message if the receiver never "understood" it. The tree may have fallen in the woods and it may have made a significant amount of noise, but what difference did that make if it was never heard? I would imagine the Arbor Society would disagree with my analysis of "what difference it made" when trees fall, but I hope you get my point.

How often do we speak first without ever taking the time to listen to what the person asked us in the first place? And then we are forced to say something like, "Oh, sorry, I thought you were asking about. . . ." instead. Society likes to blame this incredibly rude and devastating phenomenon of not listening on the fast and hectic pace at which we operate. This may very well be the reason, but it certainly should not serve as an excuse. Just because something *is* doesn't mean it should remain that way. How often do we interrupt the person who is talking to us?

During pre-planning days (before the students came back), our faculty and staff reviewed all of Stephen Covey's seven habits. One of my teachers acted out the part of Stephen Covey coming to our school to do a seven habits site visit "just to see how the school was doing integrating the seven habits." He had planted seven teachers to answer interview questions in non-example ways. The teacher asked about "proactive" whipped

Point to Ponder Take this challenge: count how many times in one conversation you start to interrupt the other person. Hmmm . . . it might be easier to start out this little science experiment by observing a conversation (on the bus, subway, in a coffee shop, at the mall, etc.) and counting the number of times one person interrupts another. It is likely that the results will be shocking.

out a prescription bottle and exclaimed, "Yes, we give Proactive to all the children at school. One pill a day seems to calm them down." Everyone laughed. When he got to "Seek first to understand, then to be understood," he began reading a bit about that habit from the book, only to be interrupted by one of the "planted" teachers asking him questions or saying, "We already do that," before he could finish each sentence. Nobody laughed. I wonder if it's because we resemble that and it hit too close to home. Please take note: we are a school who is focusing on these habits as a mission and we still find ourselves interrupting. Again, anyone who has attended a twelve step recovery group knows that the first step is admitting that there is a problem in the first place. Only then can people begin to take ownership of what to change and how to change it. One of the questions I like to ask my faculty and staff members when they talk about ineffective and frustrating conversations with parents and co-workers is, "How is that working for you?" So many of us tend to get caught in the routine of doing the same things over and over again, hoping to have different results the next time. Unfortunately, ineffective communication skills breed ineffective relationships and the cycle continues until we make a change.

The Dance of Anger by Harriet Lerner (1985) was hugely helpful to me when I was just out of college, desperately trying to change some patterns of behavior in relationships with my parents and others. She talked about how the "dance" of inappropriate behavior continues between two people until one person consciously makes the choice to simply quit dancing and get off the dance floor. If I am engaged in a conversation with my husband or one of my teachers, and we both seem to be interrupting each other, I need to make the conscious decision to get off the dance floor. Why do we find this so difficult to do? Perhaps it is a control issue. I can't let up on my own agenda or point or I won't "win." But what have we ever won by continuing to engage in unproductive patterns of communication? How about starting to make a change and see if we feel more like winners?

Our mock-Stephen Covey found several non-examples of the seven habits, but through that experience, the faculty and staff were able to see and talk about how far we have come in applying these seven habits. I love the quote from Aristotle that says, "We are what we repeatedly do. Excellence, therefore, is not an act but a habit." What we practice, we get better at. What we get better at begins to define us. What defines us becomes our mission statement and ultimately the legacy we pass along to our children.

When interviewing new teachers, I like to include two other teachers (the grade level chairperson from that particular grade level and one other support person such as our Literacy Coach, Guidance Counselor, or Media Specialist) to assist in the process. Certainly, we ask all the "usual suspect" questions such as, "Tell us about your 90-minute literacy block and what it looks like and sounds like," and, "How do you incorporate technology into your lesson plans for various curriculum areas?" But I would be lying if I told you those were the most important ones. In order to become part of a culture where communication is valued, I believe we must ask for it, demand it, and teach about it. Therefore, we ask questions of interviewees that help us determine whether or not the candidate is willing to grow in this area: "Tell us about a time you experienced miscommunication, what happened, and how you resolved it."

In seeking first to understand, we must first believe that the other person has a point that is worth hearing. Let's be perfectly honest. Have you ever had a conversation with a parent or teacher during which you believed you already knew the answer but were simply giving lip service to asking for their opinion or listening to what they had to say on the subject? Of course. Again, though, just because we have all done it does not

Point to Ponder What is your favorite interview question? Why? What does it tell you about the candidates you are interviewing?

make it right. One principal I know told me he sometimes just has to "fake it 'til he makes it," meaning he fakes listening to people until he actually is doing it.

The point is that if we actually give other people a chance to be heard, we may learn something that we had not ever intended. But I can't spend the whole time they are talking waiting (impatiently) to say what I want to say.

One of the other activities I do when I teach leadership lessons in the classrooms is to allow the students to experience the phenomenon of not being understood. I start out the lesson by setting up this scenario:

> Pretend that tomorrow morning, a new student walks into your classroom. His name is Gabe and the teacher seats him right next to you. Your job is to ensure that he knows the routine in the classroom and the way we do things around here. You turn to Gabe and you say, "I will show you where to put your lunch number when we get to the cafeteria, okay?" Gabe looks straight at you then turns his head away from you. What are you thinking?

Someone in the class inevitably pipes up with, "Maybe Gabe is just a snob," or, "Maybe he doesn't want to make friends yet," or, "Maybe Gabe is just shy," to all of which I reply, "Maybe, but what if that isn't what is going on? What else could it be?" One child (and I can never accurately predict which student it will be although I get to know the students pretty well by the first part of the year) will always tentatively guess, "Maybe Gabe is hearing-impaired and he didn't hear you," to which I jump up and down with excitement or go hug on that child and say, "Kiss your brain. You sought first to understand!"

I then present a second scenario, such as:

Pretend that tomorrow morning a new student comes in your classroom. She walks in the door and you can immediately smell that she is not clean. Her clothes look and smell dirty and you are not thrilled when the teacher puts her next to you. What do you think is going on?

One or two students might squirm or say, "Ewww . . . yuck," but remarkably, several usually raise their hands to guess something like, "Maybe they don't have running water at their house," or, "Maybe they are homeless—we are lucky to have homes so we should be nice to her anyway," to which I jump up and down and throw mock kisses at them and say, "If I ever come in a classroom, dirty and smelling not-so-winter-fresh, I hope I meet friends like you guys."

These scenarios are appropriate to any age level. Some middle school students, in an effort to belong, can often be harsh and cruel to other students who might be easy targets to pick on. But when asked in a whole group setting what they could do to seek first to understand, students will also rise to the occasion and name some insightful ideas of how to better understand a newcomer. Now, if we can just get them to apply that once they walk out the door, we'll be set.

What I have found is that giving students experiences in learning *how* to seek first helps them do a better job of it in the future. The same goes for our faculties and staffs. The more we talk and learn about understanding, the better we understand.

While I haven't done research on this phenomenon yet, I would venture to guess that most disagreements occur when we don't listen to each other fully or consider what the other person might be going through.

At the beginning of this year, right before pre-planning, our air conditioning went out. It wasn't something that could be repaired. Our fifty year old chiller had given up the ghost. Naturally, these things don't occur when it is 75 degrees outside. It was 98 degrees outside and 400% percent humidity (slight exaggeration possible). While our maintenance department worked tirelessly to procure another chiller from three states away as quickly as humanly possible, we had to alter our meeting place and times for pre-planning and professional development.

Point to Ponder How can you incorporate the scenarios above to help your faculty and staff "seek first to understand"? How about asking staff to seek first to understand the limitations of some parents who might not have the same resources as others?

I don't want to brag too much, but suffice it to say that all of the faculty and staff still got their rooms ready for Open House despite the intense heat. However, when I needed to steal my Literacy Coach from a meeting she was supposed to attend so she could present to the faculty for an hour on our adjusted day and time, I met with resistance. A specialist from the county office said, "She has to attend this meeting. She can't come to yours," and then she walked out abruptly, muttering, "I have to go now," without saying goodbye.

All I could think was that she didn't understanding how much we had already had to adapt to the heated conditions at our school. Instead, conditions were bound to heat up more if I didn't just say, "We'll work it out," and leave it. In this scenario, as an outsider looking in, I can see that from my perspective, I had a difficult time understanding why someone couldn't see that 1) we are really hot and we are having to make accommodations in our schedules and 2) I was asking for one hour of my literacy coach's time to present a much-needed hour of instruction. From the specialist's perspective, she couldn't understand 1) why my problem had to become her problem and 2) why I couldn't see that four principals had already told her their literacy coaches wouldn't be at her meeting.

What I said out loud to the people who overheard her outburst and complained that she wasn't very professional was, "I think we have to remember first and foremost that we are the 'straw that broke the camel's back' in this situation." Has this ever happened to you? Fifteen teachers come to you to ask if they can miss a meeting or if you're okay with them being late, then the sixteenth comes to you and you react as if he or she is the sixteenth one. "What?! This is important and I need everyone there!" we rant. In reality, though, we have to remember that it is only his or her first time to ask us that question. It is not fair for us to react as if that sixteenth teacher is the straw.

One of our new parents complained that she overheard something unprofessional occur out on our front doorstep on the first day of school. I was immediately mortified. What could she have witnessed? I wondered. The description she gave the teacher was, "I was hiding in the bushes to make sure my son got into school okay and that someone would take care of him. One blonde lady came out and nicely started to ask him if he needed help finding his class. But then a dark-haired lady came out and scolded the blonde lady and told her she wasn't in the right place and that she would take care of things outside. Is this the way you all do things at your school?" I immediately realized what had happened but I couldn't "catch it" before the mom went home, called the daycare and emailed the teacher. Our "blonde" music teacher and "dark-haired" guidance counselor both have front door duty. Our music teacher, however, had recently been diagnosed with Stage Four cancer in her lungs. Strong as she has been, we had altered a few things to ensure she didn't get overheated or overly stressed. Instead of meeting the children outside, she was told to hang out inside to meet and greet the children. This mom caught my guidance counselor playfully scolding her for venturing outside. I'm going to be honest. My first reaction was one of frustration. "Really?" I wanted to ask, "You really needed to hide in the bushes?" My next thought was, "Really, you felt you needed to make a big deal of that?" Instead, I asked the guidance counselor and music teacher to clear things up for the mom the next morning. Mom was sufficiently mortified, not for misunderstanding, but for acting on her misinterpretation of the entirely innocent situation. We could only be so critical before we realized that we have all done this at one time or another. We make assumptions from our own perceptions of the situation. We see things using our own particular "lens" and it distorts the way we view people, places, and situations.

So, how do we ensure that we don't make irrational decisions? One method is to bounce ideas off of another person. I think each principal needs another person who can be a confidential sounding board. If we make it a best practice to tell another principal what situation is bugging us and what we are planning to do about it, we may likely hear whether or not it is a reasonable thought and decision. An objective eye has 20/20 vision compared to a subjective one.

Some ideas for increasing your "seek first" skill base include:

- ◆ Allow teachers and teacher leaders to vent first before expecting them to move toward solutions.
- ◆ Honestly try putting yourself in the other person's shoes. Try filling in the blank of this sentence: "I might feel the same way she does if _____."
- ◆ Seek out a fellow school leader off of whom you can bounce ideas. Having an objective other can help us not take ourselves so seriously and get a fresh perspective from which to view our current situation.

In seeking first to understand, we are acknowledging that we are not the only ones with thoughts, feelings, and opinions, and that other people around us might actually have ideas and concerns that are worthy of our listening time. Like so many other skills, most of us find that the more we practice this skill, the better we will become at it.

5

One-on-One Conversations

About Data and Student Achievement

If our local grocery store wants to know if a particular brand of cereal is selling better than another brand, they will do some data analysis to figure out the answer. Perhaps they will count the number of boxes that are sold in a week's time and compare it to sales of another. At the end of the week or month, that data will show which brand the store needs to keep in stock more than the other. This data analysis is a pretty effective method for getting the answers that are needed. Why, then, do we as educators seem to balk about analyzing data from our students and using it to drive our instruction? Furthermore, why do we find it so difficult to talk about student data with each other? Perhaps the problem lies in the terminology we use. For instance, if I say to the teachers at my school, "I would like for you to do an action research project to determine on a scatter-plot what the least appropriate day of the week is for your class to do an important homework assignment," many teachers will break into a cold, clammy sweat before I am finished with the sentence and the challenge. If, however, I asked teachers to tell me what day many of their students fail to turn in homework, they could answer the question in a moment's notice. Why? Because teachers know what they know but they don't always know why they know it. Educational researchers contend that constructivist learners do the same thing. Each learner creates his own meaning, but the learners can't always explain why they know what they know.

Principals, as instructional leaders, must be willing to have courageous conversations with teachers about the need to know why they know what they know. In the age of accountability, educators must be willing to count, analyze graphs, disaggregate group test scores, plot frequencies, and so much more. If I tell you that 92% of our 4th graders passed the Florida writing test, it is because I have taken their individual scores and analyzed them. In order for teachers to have meaningful conversations with parents about their child's progress, they simply must be able to communicate the differences between percentages correct on a test and a percentile ranking. Why? Because it matters. And if teachers can't communicate it, they likely don't understand it themselves.

So, what is the answer? A quick exit card from a brief faculty meeting could determine how many of your teachers know what the difference is between a raw score, a scale score, and a stanine. Another could tell precisely how many teachers know what formative and summative assessments are and how to use each of them to direct student learning. If these statistics are pertinent in your district or county, simply ask the question and have each teacher write an answer on an index card. If 95% of the teachers get the question correct, no need for remedial tutoring on that particular topic. But if they don't understand, how can we expect them to explain test scores to parents? Knowledge is powerful and parent/teacher relationships increase in value when there is a mutual language on which both parties can agree.

About Teacher Evaluations

As a doctoral student this past semester, twenty-two of my cohort classmates and I conducted a group dissertation. The research questions were about meaningful evaluations. Although not all the data have been collected to date, the results so far are indicating that over 50% of the teachers we surveyed do not find their annual evaluations either motivating or meaningful in encouraging them to change to better teaching practices in the classroom. In fact, some respondents actually indicated that their administrator doesn't even go over the teacher evaluations with them. Some simply put the paperwork in the teachers' mailboxes and ask them to "sign and return." How can this be? Isn't the purpose of an evaluation to help us improve? When I first became a principal seven years ago, I told the faculty right upfront that they shouldn't ever expect to get a "perfect" rating on their observation/evaluation. After all, I explained, I knew that I wasn't perfect and there is always something we can work on or improve. If I simply watch teachers teach a 30-minute lesson, tell them what they did great, then we sign off on the paperwork, isn't that just a waste of my time and theirs as well?

Our county previously used a form that had two sides: the left side held the "positive" indicators for effective teaching while the right side housed the "weaker" choices in instruction. Try as I might that first year to start by telling the teacher something good that I observed in their lesson, their eyes inevitably would sweep (swoosh!) over to that right side. "What did I do wrong?" they would ask themselves, even if they didn't ask me out loud. And just like I can't focus on anything else if I am hungry (Maslow's hierarchy at its finest), they couldn't focus on anything I had to say until they saw what was marked on the right side. So, I take the bull by the horns and begin my post-observation conferences in the following way: when the teacher comes in and gets seated, I ask something trivial like, "How has your morning been so far?" then I ask the teacher to tell me how he/she thinks the lesson went. More often than not, they recognize many of the same things I noticed. Getting their input before I begin mine is important. I don't allow them to beat themselves up and I encourage them to tell me more than "good" or "not so great." After the teacher gives me feedback, I begin with "two kisses and a wish," a strategy we have stolen in teaching that provides a fair but positive critique of someone's work. The premise behind it is that for every two positive things you say, you can criticize one other thing and still be heard. Again, what is the point in slamming someone to the ground with negative feedback if they are not going to hear anything past the first couple of words?

I try to use the rule of thumb in post-observation conferencing that I should treat teachers the way I wish to be treated. I do not want my Superintendent to sugar-coat anything she has

Point to Ponder How do you handle your teacher evaluations? What are your own strengths and weaknesses in guiding teachers through their own professional development and improvement?

to tell me. I want to know in a straight-forward but fair manner what I need to work on, but I also want the courtesy of first being able to identify my areas of weakness on my own, allowing me some ownership to my own progress. One of the definitions of "Be Proactive" that we use in teaching about Stephen Covey's (1989) first habit of highly effective people is: if you control your own behavior, no one else ever has to do it for you. If a teacher can come in my office and identify his/her areas of strength and weakness in an effective manner, what more do I need to add? I think what frustrates so many teachers (and others of us as well, I can only imagine) is being beaten over the head with new mandates to which we must adhere. After a time, it simply becomes exhausting and we are either worn down into submission or we rise up in anger, neither of which is particularly productive in a school setting.

Whether your district does a formal or informal version of classroom walkthroughs, these are another source of either effective or frustrating communication between teacher and principal. After you do several walkthroughs, ask yourself the following questions:

- ◆ Do I give teachers feedback?
- ◆ How do I give teachers feedback?
- ◆ What sort of self-reflection or metacognition do I ask my teachers to do on their own?

I know it might sound silly, but each year, I invest in loads of motivational note pads. You know the kind. I like to get ones that have inspirational teaching quotes on them as ones that simply have cute Labrador Retrievers or serene and picturesque scenes on them. Why is this the least bit important? Think of notes you have received. Have you ever felt like the message was enhanced by the type of note paper it was written on? I tend to believe it is, in the same way many believe a romantic dinner is enhanced by the candlelight and table setting that accompany the meal.

Finally, are you afraid to get rid of bad teachers? Whether you work in a district with a union or not, principals need to be willing to do what it takes to grow good teachers, improve adequate teachers, and encourage poor teachers to get out of the profession if they are unwilling or unable to show improvement. A wise man once told me, "It may be that teacher's last year before she retires, but it is definitely the 3rd grade year of each child in her classroom." I get it—it is not fair to even one child to have to spend a year's worth of time in the classroom of a less-than-adequate classroom teacher. I have often asked myself, when I am trying to decide whether or not to put a teacher on an improvement plan, "Is this classroom good enough for the children of the President of the United States?" If the answer is something like, "Are you kidding me? This classroom is not good enough for my own Labrador Retrievers," then we have a problem. After all, what about that great research study on how one year of having an ineffective teacher will likely impact a student for many years to come, possibly for the rest of their school career? Principal leaders need to be willing and able to make tough decisions.

About Parent Communication

What we reap, we sow. When it comes to teaching teachers how to communicate more effectively with parents, I honestly believe this. If administrators want to build better teacher communicators, we need to role-model the skill, talk about our successes and failures (the "glam" and the warts), and give teachers feedback when we witness their teacher/parent interactions. When the teachers at our school are asked what the most difficult part of their job is, many will say, "Dealing with difficult parents." So what do we do about it? To be perfectly honest, I think we often stick our heads in the sand and do nothing. We don't reach out to the parent who needs to hear from us. We don't find out why that parent is leaving our school

Point to Ponder The video about "eating your frog" can be found at www.eatthatfrogmovie.com. Similar videos are free to use and can be found at www.simpletruths.com. How about trying one out for your next faculty/staff meeting?

to homeschool their child. Why? I don't know for sure about you, but I for me it's because I flat-out hate confrontation.

During pre-planning this year, we watched a video clip that talked about "eating your frog." The premise is that if you eat a live frog first thing in the morning, you will have likely taken care of the worst thing you will have to do all day.

Some of us know for certain that this is not always the case. Just because you have had a horrible day does not preclude tomorrow from being an equally horrible day. There is not an "I've done my time" badge we can wear to say that we are now immune to bad things happening. This old saying about the frog is more geared to remind us that if something is looming over our heads, nasty as the task seems, we should jump in and take care of it. Stephen Covey's (1989) first habit of highly effective people says we should be proactive. What more proactive stance than to take care of difficult tasks as they arise?

On the second day of school, one of our brand new students "lost" his lunch. As irony would have it, the fourth graders had just begun reading a story entitled "The Case of the Missing Lunch," but irony alone will not console a child who is missing his lunchbox. Naturally, we got him a lunch from the cafeteria and found out shortly after lunch that his lunch had been eaten by another fourth grade boy who, remarkably, didn't remember he hadn't brought his lunch that day. As "Dillon" was new to our school, we had no prior knowledge of how his mom might react when he got home. His teacher showed extraordinary perceptive and proactive initiative by suggesting we go ahead and call the mom to tell her that Dillon had, indeed, eaten a lunch, but it hadn't exactly been the lunch she had sent in for him. We decided that eating that frog might save us some hassle in the future. The teacher felt good, the parent was fine (we didn't

> **Point to Ponder** Who among us has *not* dreaded making a phone call to a parent we know is not likely to be happy with us? What can you do to be proactive about the conversation? What do you tell yourself before you make the phone call? I have been known to say, "This, too, shall pass."

share the humorous part about the connection to the story with her, but we sure did pass that story around our own faculty for everyone's amusement), and Dillon was no worse for the wear.

Teachers need to see us make those proactive choices to call the "maybe upset parent" before the "definitely mad parent" calls us. And how we say what we say is as important as what we say, right?

About Student Discipline/Behavior

Just as our students want to please us (I really believe this and am not just saying it for the book), I think teachers want to please administrators. Obviously, some are a bit more diligent and obvious in their aim to please. Often, unless administrators are in and around the classrooms, the discipline and behavior issues facing our teachers could evade us due to the fact that teachers only show us what they want us to see. I prefer teachers to be transparent—with their expectations of the students, their relationships with parents, and their rules and classroom management strategies. I go over this at the beginning of each year: I expect teachers to expect good behavior and good choice-making from their students.

If you were asked to write down the top three classroom managers in your school, could you do it without thinking too hard? What about if you were asked to write down the last three that would make your list—the least effective classroom managers? Of course you know who these folks are because, over time, principals come to expect that the bulk of their discipline referrals will likely come from the same small percentage

Point to Ponder Can you think of an effective way to say this to a teacher who might be somewhat sensitive to parent complaints about behavior?

of teachers. Are there exceptions? Of course there are. But take a minute to think back to the last ten parent concerns you have addressed. Do you see a pattern?

When it comes to behavior, teachers need to accept only what they expect—nothing more and nothing less. Unfortunately, this means something different to each teacher. When asked to establish a classroom management plan, I expect teachers to talk about Harry Wong and possibly Doug Lemov, another great guru of procedures and expectations. Some folks will write their expectations in the classroom and possible real-world consequences if the students don't comply. But inevitably, a few teachers will write down a discipline plan that lays out all the rules and negative consequences in big, bold letters with no regard to how respectful it sounds. Discipline plans should be guidelines for students to operate effectively in the classroom. Many teachers like to develop their plans on the first day of school in conjunction with the students. Can the teacher have certain must-haves? Sure thing; but the buy-in from students can make all the difference in the world when reminding the students what they all agreed to.

So, how can principals best help teachers deal with behavioral issues if the teacher is not 100% strong in this area or seems to rely on negative reinforcement more than positive? I like to use the approach of giving helpful hints like, "Several teachers have told me that they have had success with the following management strategies:. . . ." In other words, we're sharing knowledge. I have also found, through experience, that most teachers are human and don't like to be "called out" for their own downfalls. In other words, I try in every way possible not to give too much negative feedback like, "You need to quit talking so loudly to your students. It scares them." And I never, ever, ever (except when I forget and do this and then regret that

I did it) tell a teacher, "Several parents are complaining that you are way too loud in the classroom."

A better technique might be to say something like, "What do you do to lower your speaking voice when you find yourself getting too loud to the point that you might be intimidating a child?" Wording the question like this does three things:

♦ It allows the teacher to problem solve him/herself instead of the principal telling her what to do.
♦ It takes the blame and accusation away.
♦ It gives the true impression that the administrator wants to help solve the problem.

I always make sure to tell parents during Open House that if they come to see me or call me regarding a teacher/child concern, I will always refer them to the teacher first. I do this out of respect for the teacher and to encourage parent/teacher communication. To date, I have not had a parent complaint about this policy. Everyone seems to understand and respect "chain of command."

Expectations, rules, procedures, and routines are so crucial to a classroom's well-being. The beginning of the school year is the time to ensure the fidelity of the management for the rest of the school year. For this reason, when I talk to teachers about their first week's lesson plans, I tell them to include as much Harry Wong as they can into the first week before delving into subject matter. What good will come from content taught in an ill-managed classroom? We must take care of first things first.

About Expectations—What You Expect, You Accept

Doug Lemov's book *Teach Like a Champion* (2010) suggests that teachers should give students the benefit of the doubt when expecting participation, procedure adherence, and respect for the class. In other words, the teacher should not assume that a child who doesn't put his homework folder out on his desk like the teacher asked is acting defiantly. Perhaps that child honestly can't remember which folder is the homework folder. The strategy to employ, therefore, is to say something like, "I'm waiting until everyone remembers to get out the red homework folder that has a picture of a house on the front and puts it on their desk. I think we are still missing one." How different does this sound than, "Jeffrey, which word in my last request did you *not* understand?" Have you ever heard such a thing? Well, of course you have, but hopefully you haven't heard it twice.

Assuming that the issue is one of ignorance, forgetfulness, or not hearing instead of noncompliance allows the tone to be lighter in the classroom. What then shall we do with the teacher who doesn't turn in lesson plans by the due date? What should we say to the one teacher who didn't show up in the lunchroom on the first day when you asked every teacher to come eat lunch with the children? Why not try the same technique? Therefore, when three or four teachers have not turned in their lesson plans to you, which will you say?

a. "Lesson plans were due yesterday—look in your handbook if you need a reminder of the rules. I expect everyone to comply with them."
b. "Just a quick reminder that I am missing a copy of your lesson plans."
c. "Hello. . . . . did you forget something???"

No, no, no—not "a." Teachers are professional and don't want to be beaten over the head with guilt. And "c" seems slightly condescending. How about "b"?

Recently, I had the opportunity to try this on for size. I had asked each teacher to spend the first three days in the cafeteria during their lunchtime. The time spent those first three days on routines and procedures is worth its weight in solid gold. Unfortunately, one of my teachers didn't come to the cafeteria. I thought about it that night and wondered, "What should I say?" What if I told her I expected her in there just like everyone else—after all, we're a team and everyone should do their part—and she told me to go take a hike? Instead, I did what Doug Lemov suggested. In fact, I confronted her *with* Doug Lemov. I caught up with her on the bus ramp the next morning and said, "You know what Doug Lemov says about assuming that students sometimes don't do things out of defiance but instead out of ignorance for the expectation? I am wondering if the same thing has happened here with the request for teachers to come in the cafeteria for the first three days of school." A hand slapped over her forehead (her hand, not mine), and she exclaimed, "Shoot! I knew I forgot to do something! Yes, I will be there today! Sorry!" Wow! How would that conversation have turned out differently if I would have said something like, "Hey, everyone else is doing their fair share coming to the cafeteria. Do you have a problem with it or something?" I assumed that it was a mistake and it was a mistake. Do we administrators want to *be* right or do we want to *make it* right? If we look at our motives and we honestly want a school that communicates with less tension, we need to talk to people the way we would want to have people talk to us.

Therefore, whether the discussion that needs to take place with the teacher is about data, student achievement, parent concerns, a poor evaluation, or a need for improved classroom management, we school leaders need to stand up strong and face what we need to do. We must be careful not to think we are simply being nice and polite by not confronting what needs to be confronted. It is neither nice nor polite to avoid telling people what they need to hear. John Maxwell said, "If we're growing, we're always going to be out of our comfort zone." Let's grow!

6

Avoid Defensiveness

Why do we let the little things get to us? Think back to the last time you lost your cool or broke into a bit of a sweat while conversing with one of your teachers. Why do you think it happened? Stress can cause us to react in ways that we normally wouldn't under "calm" conditions. But if we are being honest, each one of us has likely reacted in ways that we might not want documented by radio, film, television, or press. Stephen Covey's (1989) seventh habit is "Sharpen the Saw." I like to personally think about this habit when I need to get centered or focus on the reason I went into education in the first place. What helps you get serene? A nice, hot bubble bath when you get home from work? A frozen hot chocolate from your favorite coffee establishment? A good long talk with your best friend? How about prayer and a good church service? I think all of these and many more will help administrators keep from getting defensive and frustrated with our employees.

But at one time or another, something will hit us the wrong way and we will feel compelled to lash out with anger, sarcasm, frustration or stony silence. When in doubt, pick silence, although we should try to leave the "stony" part out of the equation. It will get you in much less trouble and there will to apologize about after the fact. Eating crow doesn't taste so great but eat it we must if we have ordered a big plate of it and can't send it back.

One of the biggest challenges for administrators is dealing with people questioning the leader's judgment, authority, or information. When we stand in front of our faculty and staff and say, "We need to do formative assessments on our children this year," and one of the teachers rolls her eyes and asks with her voice dripping with derision, "Why do we have to test kids so much? Everyone knows that too much testing is not good for children," what is your initial reaction? If you are reading this, thinking that your answer is, "To spin out of control and screw myself into the ceiling," perhaps you might be a bit defensive. I have felt that before. "Why are you questioning my authority?" I want to shout. I learned the hard way that the least effective answer to a question such as this was, "Because the powers that be at the state level are making us." Not only does this diminish, rather than increase our authority (oh well, we just have to do what they say), it implies that we don't believe it's the right thing to do for children and we're only doing it because *they said so*. Is this what you really want your teachers to believe? So, how shall we react instead? Maybe the best tactic is to react in the way in which you would honestly want to be treated when the shoe is on the other foot. "I know it seems frustrating, but formative assessments should be driving our instruction and they have helped us make great leaps in the last few years. The good news is: when we begin them, we are going to make sure you have a half-day substitute to help you get all this testing in." I know a principal who says, "Let's just put on our big girl panties on and get it done." I couldn't say that to the teachers at my school. The point is: you know your teachers—what do they want to hear? What do you feel comfortable saying to them?

At the end of the day, what do you want? I want for everyone to be ready to rise to the challenge of making education at our school a positive experience—for the students, for the parents, for each other, and for ourselves. With that being my own personal goal, I must admit that my feathers get ruffled by those who would disturb the progressive nature in our school. If teachers are content with "status quo," if they believe that being a squeaky wheel is the best way to get something done, and particularly if they feel the need to air someone else's laundry to others who don't have a need to know, I admit to getting a bit defensive. So, how do we combat that? If I know these are some of my triggers, then I simply need to be proactive about dealing with them. I reward teachers who think outside the box, who are solution-minded and who come up with positive ideas versus hurtful comments. When I get the chance, I reward those folks at faculty and staff meetings with a gift card to a

Point to Ponder What are your pet peeves when it comes to communication with teachers? Can you name them? Can you identify concrete strategies to deal with them?

local restaurant. Teachers can even nominate other teachers or staff members for going above and beyond, and the nominee gets recognized as well as the nominator. It may not seem like much, but who doesn't like receiving a token treat for going above and beyond? Besides, you're once again drawing attention to the desired behaviors you want and expect.

Therefore, in order to do the above, administrators must figure out their pet peeves and the things that get under their skin and stay in touch with them.

Administrators must be the calm in the storm for the rest of their faculty and staff or else the storm will envelop the entire school and reign down chaos upon the universe. Okay, perhaps that might be a tiny bit dramatic, but there is a hint of truth to it, isn't there? If you aren't calm and cool, how can you expect your staff to stay that way? When our air conditioning went out in 98 degree August weather right before school began, I made sure our maintenance folks had the new chiller headed our way and then I told the staff, "We will be okay." I honestly believe that a couple of the teachers wanted me to freak out. "Do they know how hot it is in here?" they wanted to know. "What will happen if it's not working in the morning when the kids come back to school?" I was reminded of Scarlett O'Hara asking, "Where will I go? What will I do?" I know this to be true: there can only be one crazy person at a time. Someone has to keep their sanity, and I hope it is usually me.

We have all likely employed the "don't let the kids see you sweat" tactic, but do teachers sometimes make you feel like you need to put on stronger deodorant? If so, it might be necessary to learn to control some of that frustration. Carrie Underwood sings a song about how someone "took away my happy" and all I can think anytime I hear that song is that she needs to not give up her happy to anyone. Is it worth it for me to wake up at 2:00 in the morning because I am frustrated with someone? "No, no, no," the answer is "no," and don't you forget it. You're only letting that person live, rent-free, in your head. It's not worth it! Now, don't get me wrong. I have *lots* of 2:00 in the morning moments in which I have an epiphany, an idea that simply cannot rest easily inside my brain until the next morning. It awakens me with a bolt of lightning and says to me, "You must act on this amazing idea immediately." In fact, some of the teachers at my school joke with me and say, "Hey, you must have woken me up last night—I had a 2:00 in the morning moment, too." I keep a notebook beside my bed for those times.

But it is a wholly different thing to be awakened with a resentment against someone who has either embarrassed, frustrated, or otherwise "wronged" you. Who, I have to ask myself, is the one who is sitting up in bed fuming about the interaction we had earlier that day and who is in bed? There is a funny saying I like to use in workshops that says, "Never mud-wrestle with a pig. You only end up muddy and the pig loves it." Pretty good advice, right? Unless I enjoy getting muddy, I should avoid getting into the pigpen with any pigs. Some people simply enjoy or thrive on confrontation. I think it goes back to the question of whether you want to be right or you want to make it right. I may not ever be able to change other people, but I certainly don't have to engage in that negative behavior myself. Instead, I can take care of myself and make sure that I don't end up acting in ways that I will regret later on.

When I was in college, I sang in several choirs. My choir director was a fabulous musician and a man of few words. When we were practicing a new piece of music in our 16-person a cappella group, one of us would sometimes sing the part incorrectly. "Dr. Chamberlain," we would announce, "we just sang that part wrong." His succinct words of musical wisdom would consist of, "Bad. Don't do that again." The point is: if I'm doing something that is counterproductive to relationships and communication, the simplest solution is "Don't do it again." Why commit the act of insanity by doing the same thing over and over again, hoping against hope that maybe, just maybe, the insane thing won't produce insane results just this one time?

More than likely, defensiveness usually rears its ugly head when we feel as though someone is trying to blame *us* for the

Point to Ponder Do you ever wallow around with the pigs in the pigpen and then later complain that your clothes are dirty? How can you avoid that?

situation in which they find themselves. So, when a teacher comes to you saying her room is too cold, the natural response might be, "I'm so sorry, I will get Maintenance to come check it out for you." But if, three days later, the room still feels as though you could hang meat in it and it is February, the teacher's comment, "Is it ever going to get fixed?" likely strikes a chord of blame in your heart. Instead of reacting by saying, "I can totally see why you are frustrated," you respond instead by saying, "Hey, don't yell at me," or, "Hey, I've called it in. I can't help it if they haven't come yet." Okay, we really don't say those things, but we might think them.

Have you ever met someone who didn't ever get defensive? I am in awe of people who can take someone's sarcastic comments or personal digs and continue to say, "Well, I can see how you could think that, but . . ." I might be able to do that sometimes when all the stars are in proper alignment, but ultimately I am going to have to tell that person that I felt that their comments were hurtful. But what shall we do when that person is one of our teachers? Should we tell them they hurt our feelings? Should we tell them they are being insubordinate? Should we execute them on the spot? Oh dear, how did that slip in? The "line" is a blurry one and school leaders often find themselves straddling the fence and wondering about the right thing to do.

A good trick of the trade is to take responsibility for that which you can take responsibility and let go of that which you cannot. In other words, if I told a teacher I would do something and I forgot, it pays in huge dividends to admit my error and say, "I'm sorry for letting you down." If, however, the teacher accuses me of being a cheerleader for the district when they are advocating a new program that isn't popular among teachers, I may say something like, "I am sorry you feel that way, but I think we have a responsibility to do what's best for children and this is worth trying out." A teacher once told me, "I will never again apologize to a parent if I didn't do anything wrong because they will only take that and use it against me for ammunition." Yikes! My theory is this: apologizing for something I did or didn't do is crucial for maintaining good relationships with other people. On the other hand, if something has occurred in school or in a classroom that was out of my control, I can still say, "I am so sorry that happened," without accepting blame to the point of asking for a beating. I think we should be aware of the difference and be willing to do or say what we need to in order to solve the problem. Ultimately, we will act or react in a way that reflects how we answer that question, "Do I want to be right or do I want to make it right?"

Some people just seem to be hard-wired to think that others are out to get them. In a helping profession such as education, this seems a bit incongruous. But I have seen this phenomenon quite a few times and it is a very difficult attitude to combat. Teachers who operate under this premise are constantly under the impression that parents, other staff, and maybe even the administrator are separately or all at once out to get them.

As with any other feeling or attitude, much of this defensiveness is "normal" and "human." After all, we probably developed a defensive nature in order to protect us like armor would protect a knight in battle. A fellow counselor once shared that she tells her clients that we all need to do a better job of acting like our exteriors are made of Teflon. To be honest, while I know this would be healthier for me to do, I sometimes find this incredibly difficult to do. Perhaps my non-stick coating has become defective. All I know is I am the only one who can protect myself from feeling defensive to the point of being ineffective. When that happens, I must step back and take a good hard look at what is and is not so important.

Techniques to Avoid Defensiveness

So what do you do when you start to feel your face getting red and flushed with defensiveness and anger? I suggest the following:

- It may be overused, but its impact is not overrated—TAKE A DEEP BREATH. A teacher I know who likes to spin out of control now says to me, as she is about to pull her hair out with anxiety, "I know, deep cleansing breaths. Deep cleansing breaths." I know that she is, in a way, making fun or mocking my simple advice to her to take deep cleansing breaths, but guess what she is doing in between saying this? Taking deep cleansing breaths!

- Know your triggers and prepare for them. If you know that heat, fatigue, hunger, or thirst can add to your frustration, by all means keep the granola bars handy for those times that a teacher wants to meet with you and you can't get lunch. A diet coke with crushed ice is my worst vice but it can get me through a tough afternoon.

- I believe a famous country song says, "You say it best when you say nothing at all." When in doubt, never pass up an opportunity to remain silent when you are frustrated. Opening my mouth when I am angry typically results in demonstrating my anger. Be sure, however, to reserve a time and place to vent later or those ugly feelings will likely find a way to creep out at the most unlikely or undesirable time.

7

Let's Not Call the
Whole Thing Off . . . Yet

Knowing what to say and how to say it can be a daunting task at best. However, when the going gets tough, how do you know when to issue a final ultimatum to a teacher? Despite sometimes feeling defensive, we all know when we have reached the point at which we are "past the point of no return," to quote a line from "Phantom of the Opera." We want to throw in the towel, trade in our tattered cheerleading pom-poms for a new line of work, or retire early. Communication and relationship issues can cause fatigue in a principal quicker than anything else. Early on in the principalship, heated discussions and a bout of dissension between a few teachers about a tender subject that was near and dear to all of them took place. We finally convinced everyone who was so passionate about the issue to "agree to disagree." One of my very vocal teachers came up to me after a faculty meeting at which I had told everyone a bit of budget woes, and said, "That must be the worst part of your job—deciding how best to budget for staff and supplies when we keep getting less and less money." I only paused for an instant before shaking my head and saying, "No, I can deal with any budget constraints the state throws at me. I can deal with any policy changes our county throws at us. What I cannot stand is watching staff members tear each other apart." That will drop me to my knees more quickly than anything.

But it happens. We say things that hurt. We hurt each other with our words. People say and do things that cause permanent riffs between them. Who among us has not had an issue with a parent, child, sibling, or other family member that could have potentially severed the relationship? We have to ask ourselves if the pain we have experienced from fighting or disagreeing with another is worth giving up on the relationship. And, at the end of our days, are we truly willing to accept that we didn't at least try to make amends with the person? Families of origin can truly be a pain to deal with, but aren't those relationships worth it? Don't we have something to gain from maintaining those relationships?

And yet, sometimes it seems as though we work and work on relationships and communication all for naught. People don't respond the way we think they should. Over the years as principal, I have had this happen with a teacher or two. The relationship seemed to go like this: I would try to say "hello" or "good morning" and get a minimal response. I'd strike up a casual conversation as we passed in the hallway. She would respond and I would think we were making headway. The next day, she would come in my office, griping about something that was clearly beyond my control (or hers, for that matter). She'd end up storming out of my office, huffing and puffing. Everyone in the school seemed to complain that she was so very difficult to like or to work with. Once, I confronted her to say, "I know you aren't happy here. Perhaps you want to consider changing schools. Maybe a principal at another school wouldn't encourage you to get along with everyone like I do." "Whoa!" she said as she sat back in her chair. "Are you telling me to get out of this school?" Oh how I wished I could have just said "Yes." Unfortunately or fortunately, depending on how you look at it, I really like my job and I opted to say instead, "I just want you to consider doing something that might make you happier." As quick as a flash, she jumped up from the chair and hissed, "Maybe I don't want to be happy." Now, there's a new one, I thought. If someone truly doesn't want to be happy or doesn't know how to be happy, how am I (little old me!) going to change that? So, I made the toughest decision of my professional career. As if I had been holding on to the rope tied to the last lifeboat from the Titanic, I just let go. I let go.

The end of the year came and went.

That August, we started back to school and yes, she still walked in the door the first day of pre-planning. That was the year we began talking about Stephen Covey's seven habits. We had a guest speaker who talked, along with me, about making a paradigm shift—changing the way we viewed the world. If we wanted something to get done, the guest speaker suggested, perhaps we needed to quit blaming or assuming others should do it and maybe, just maybe, we needed to just get in there and do what needed to be done. Her example included those times that we walk in the restroom and see water all over the sink. "Now, why doesn't someone clean that up? How disgusting is that?" She said her attitude changed when she decided, instead of complaining about what others weren't doing, to do something herself. She said she picked up a paper towel and wiped away the water and her life has literally changed because of that choice. Many head-nods were seen throughout the morning's session.

Somewhere, about mid-morning that first day back at school, I began to notice a change. That formerly anti-social teacher began to talk with other teachers. She participated in a group discussion/debate we had about the practice of assigning and grading homework. And she laughed!

I had let go and here she was, swimming back on the raft. How had that happened? Maybe it had a little to do with my letting go, quitting trying to control everybody and everything in my sight. But who knows? Maybe she also had a change of heart and was working to try to make a paradigm shift in her own life as well.

Everyone has someone who is the caretaker of the faculty. You know who I mean—the one who dries teachers' tears, puts sweet notes in teachers' boxes, and keeps up with everyone's birthdays. Every school has an angel such as this. A few years ago, the angel came to me to tell me that every time she put up birthdays, one of the teachers would take down her own birthday notice. Finally, the angel had had enough. Even angels sometimes lose a tiny bit of loft from their wings when they are pushed around for too long. She came in my office and said, "I put everyone's birthdays up on the board and Susan keeps taking hers down. If she doesn't want to be recognized, she has won. I will not ever again put a card in her box or acknowledge her birthday on the board." Wow, it's true. We just can't please everyone, can we? When do you realize this relationship isn't going anywhere?

But then someone or something comes along to make us keep focused on what is important. One of the teachers was diagnosed with Stage 4 cancer in her lungs last year. She was given one to two years to live. When we began school this year, I asked if anyone had gone anywhere fun or had any exciting news to share with the group. The teacher jumped up from her seat and said, "I do! I got my report back from the doc yesterday and I am in *remission!*" You see, there is hope. Hearing something like this puts things in perspective. How important is that thing that we can't even remember made us so mad last week when lives are at stake?

"Calling the whole thing off" also means knowing when to fight the battle or to let it go. How big of a deal is this? Teachers often ask their kids who come to them complaining of multiple issues throughout the day, "Are you bleeding or is there something broken?" I have to remember to do the same. In the whole scheme of things, how much does this issue matter? From the 50,000 foot perspective, how big of a deal is this?

One principal I knew used to tell his faculty and staff that schools were like different cruise ship lines. They all offer something different—some are more child-centered than others; some have more amenities; some require a stricter dress code, etc. This principal would stand in front of his faculty and staff and "invite" folks to leave if they wanted to change cruise lines: "There are lots of choices out there. You might not want to sail on this one anymore, and that's okay with me if you don't. But if you choose to sail, these are the expectations on this particular cruise line."

Another principal I know sets out transfer request forms at the time of her annual evaluations to encourage people to apply for a transfer to another school if they are not happy with what is going on at their current school. While I understand this, I am not certain that it suits me or what I stand for and believe in.

Administrators set the tone for a school, every day, every interaction, all day. If we take a negative stance from the onset of an encounter with our teachers, then what does that say? The same principal told me that she recently got fed up with low budgets, class size restrictions, new unfunded mandates, and started an argument with a county administrator over the phone. She said when she was done with the argument, she hung up the phone, picked up her purse, walked out of her office, and called out to all those who were listening (and let's

Point to Ponder What do you say to your faculty and staff to encourage them to be team players? How well do your faculty and staff members play together?

review—our faculty and staff members are always listening to us, really!), "I quit! I've had it! I'm done!" and then she walked out of the building, got in her car, and drove home. Of course she went back the next day (mostly, she said, because her family just bought a new boat that she wants to get paid off), but to what end? I wonder what damage we do when we show all of our frustration to everyone in shouting distance. If we want our teachers to show self-control and restraint in their conversations with parents and students, shouldn't we do the same with our teachers? I think the teachers know that we'd be mortified to hear that they had stomped out the classroom shouting, "I quit!" or, "Take this job and shove it!" so I figure we better not do the same.

The following questions should put the issue in perspective.

◆ *What is the issue?* First of all, make sure that the issue you think is an issue is actually the issue. A few years ago, members of the teachers' union were asking a teacher questions about her certification and number of hours she worked, etc. Thinking that perhaps these union members were trying to prove the teacher ineffective, the principal questioned one of them. The union member quickly informed the principal they just wanted to invite this teacher to join the union and needed to verify that she was a full-time teacher in order to do so. Sometimes we make a mountain out of a molehill when we should really just leave it right-sized.

◆ *Do I need to do something about it?* Is this an issue I need to act on? If so, I want to be as proactive as possible. I think this is where "picking your battles" comes in particularly handy. A few years ago, I had two employees who I mutually adored. It came to my attention that one of them would not talk to the other one for reasons not known to the first one. Although it was my strong desire to have everything good between them, I struggled for a couple of days about whether or not I should intervene. I came up with this rule of thumb: We are not always going to love everyone equally, but as the administrator in the school, I have an obligation to get involved if I find that an issue is creating problems big enough for others to notice or the issue begins to interfere with a person's ability to conduct their work appropriately. In this case, one employee was working *way* too hard to avoid the other so I ultimately had to intervene. We had a mediation session and worked out the misunderstandings as best we could.

- *What can I do about it?* Do I need to go into a thumb-wrestling match with a Samurai sword? Before I act on an issue with a teacher, I should make sure that I am well-armed with the correct information and not go charging in with a weapon that is too big for the fight.
- *If it is out of my control, how can I let it go?* What if it is something that is beyond my control? Do I, as a person who wants everything to be safe, serene, and happy at my school, have the capacity to let this issue go? This is probably the most difficult one for me to do. As administrators in our schools, we want so badly for things to be repaired, we try to solve problems that perhaps might be beyond solving.

Obviously, each school, district, or state has its own policies and procedures for terminating a relationship with a teacher at a particular school. As so much literature is suggesting recently, it can sometimes be very difficult to remove an incompetent teacher, much less one who is simply a poor communicator or a grumpy, negative person. But it can certainly be done, and we should never operate under the notion that, "At least that teacher is retiring in one more year" or "two more years," etc. We should be proactive in creating opportunities for teachers to examine their choice of profession if they are so unhappy and we have exhausted all our resources on this front.

8

Improving Parent/Teacher Communication From the Inside-Out

Role-Model Conference

Several years ago, I hosted an administrative intern for the summer. We had spent a good deal of time discussing good communication with parents and teachers, but I thought real-life experience would be better than mere words. However, since it was summer, I didn't have many parent or teacher conferences for her to attend. I asked a parent who is into drama to come in and role-play with me for the unsuspecting intern.

We planned our strategy one day while the intern was out of the building. The plan was for the two of us to demonstrate all the non-examples of good listening and good communication. After all, the intern had heard me talk the talk. I thought it would be helpful for her to see what happens if we don't follow through in our walk.

The drama-parent and I then scheduled our conference. I asked the intern to join us and to take notes, paying special attention to good communication skills.

The administrative intern was diligent. She came in with her pen and notebook, ready to take notes, and introductions were made. We then proceeded to make almost every communication error a principal and parent could make. As Mom expressed her concerns about her 3rd grade child having to be retained, I interrupted and was sarcastic ("You're kidding me, right?" I asked when Mom said, "We've never heard from the teacher that there was a problem."). I even called my secretary during the meeting to ask her to call me if my interior decorator called ("I am having some beautiful new drapes delivered this afternoon and I really need to talk to her. Yes," I continued talking to the secretary, "they are so pretty. I will have to show you

Point to Ponder How would a role-play depicting "what to do" and "what not to do" impact teachers more than simply telling them how they should communicate? How does it help our students to have experiences such as role-play?

the samples later . . ."). This patient intern took copious notes at first before she began to look from me to Mom with a look of complete and utter disbelief. She squirmed in her seat, looking markedly uncomfortable and finally set her notebook down on the table. Apparently, the intern had no good communication skills to observe; therefore, note-taking had become a futile task.

A few moments later, when Mom cried out in mock frustration, "Well, I never . . ." I looked at the intern and said, "And we who care about good communication would *never*," and let her know that we had set up a scenario of "what not to do." A look of sheer relief crossed her face as she sank back down into her seat and exclaimed, "Thank goodness!!" She kept reiterating that she couldn't believe that after she and I had discussed so many positive examples of communication, I would talk to a parent like I had.

We spent a good deal of time de-briefing since role-plays are extremely powerful but only if the discussion afterwards is dissected thoroughly and properly. We discussed the necessity to watch for some of those tendencies in each conversation we have with teachers or parents and how to guard against complacency in our role as administrator.

The drama-mom, the intern, and I all sat down and talked about what makes for good communication. This intern, who will soon become an administrator, experienced more than an episode of "Punk'd" or "Candid Camera." She said that despite being "tricked," she was so appreciative of the experiential practice of seeing how ineffective some of our real-life communication strategies are. "What's so amazing," she said, "is that we have all done some of those things in conferences with teachers and parents. You just happened to do them all at the same time."

Most likely, we only have a few communication habits we need to change. If we are courageous enough to do the footwork, we can likely become much better communicators who instill trust in teachers, staff, parents, and students.

Actions Speak Louder than Words

Have you ever tried to talk to a teacher while, despite your calm-looking exterior (because you never want to let them see you sweat), you are seething underneath? We learned in Psychology 101 about cognitive dissonance, that strange phenomenon in which we have two opposing thoughts or experiences at the exact same time. For instance, if I am smiling at you while you tell me your problem, but I am internally seething, you are likely going to be confused and our communication is going to suffer.

We need to model for others what we want them to do. To simply expect good communication without doing it ourselves is like trying to enforce the "No gum-chewing" policy for students while we smack away on our own. We simply can't, as educational leaders in our schools, tout one belief while acting in an opposite way. It truly does create cognitive dissonance. If teachers hear us speak one way then watch us act another way, they will likely cock their heads to the side as my Labrador Retrievers do when they hear an odd sound on the television. Our words need to be synonymous with our actions.

A great example occurred when our school decided to focus on good leadership skills. We had adopted and infused Stephen

---

Point to Ponder We principals experience cognitive dissonance when, in a meeting, we hear these two statements: "You will meet class-size next year, so you may have to hire more teachers," and, "Your budget will have $400,000 less this year," in the same 30-minute span. What other examples of cognitive dissonance have you experienced?

Point to Ponder Mirrors are great sources of information. Try saying something you need to tell someone else while you look in the mirror. What does your face say while you are talking?

Covey's *The 7 Habits of Highly Effective People*. We had read Covey's book as a book study throughout our entire school, including parents, staff and faculty. After all of the Covey training and indoctrination, how can I, then, shut a teacher down when she comes up with a suggestion for school beautification or improvement, even if I don't agree with it? Covey's fifth habit is "Seek first to understand, then to be understood." Even if I think the teacher's idea is completely insane, I must at least reserve judgment and not roll my eyes during their proposal. My husband has told me numerous times never to play poker because I would give away my hand immediately.

If you are reading this book and you decide to e-mail me with a question, I better take the time to talk to you about your concern. Otherwise, I lose all credibility with my audience. Teachers, parents, and even students are watching us all the time. You know this is true. "I saw you at Wal-Mart yesterday, Mrs. Arneson," the kids will say, as if I didn't remember. "You were moving your mouth when you were talking for the puppet on the news show, Mrs. Arneson," the kids will critique. My response to that is always the same—redirect. "Don't you just love that silly Libby the Lab?" I dare you to try wearing the same dress or pants two days in a row. They will *know*! Worse yet, they will tell you! Your teachers watch you, too. Just as much as the kids do. How we carry ourselves truly matters. If we ask our teachers not to gossip about parents or students in the hallway, then we clearly need to never be caught whispering about an annoying parent in the hallway.

We need to walk the walk and not just talk the talk. At our school, every teacher and staff member received a copy of Suzanne Capek Tingley's book *How to Handle Difficult Parents* (2006). We spent time during pre-planning learning about the different parenting types and how we as educators could better address each type (Helicopter Parent, Pinnochio's Mom, etc.).

Point to Ponder How have you used role-plays with your teachers? Don't assume your teachers are 100% comfortable with conferencing. Take some time each year to review what good communication skills are and *practice* them!

We spent the first day of our pre-planning/inservice days jigsawing the book, then we split into groups and acted out parent/teacher conferences. The conversations and discussions which ensued were riveting, to say the least. Some teachers argued, "But parents don't talk to us in this professional manner." "Yes," some others argued, "but we have to remain professional anyway because it's the right thing to do." Still others said, "Some of these parents haven't ever experienced good communication skills. What are we teaching them if we give it right back to them?" So true. The experience allowed the teachers to read, discuss, and act out information we could have tried to impart through a powerpoint presentation. But this way, the effective communication was experiential, not just didactic.

It is true that even teachers don't always talk to us in the most professional manner. It is frustrating and even embarrassing when a teacher speaks unprofessionally in the middle of a meeting that includes both parent and teacher leaders. After one such episode this past year, I spent some time that evening trying to decide the best course of action. Should I say something to her? Should I scold her for her insensitivity to other teachers and parents? Or should I let it slide? What a quandary we face. We have a choice. We can leap across our desk at teachers and throttle them while asking, "Do you want to say that again?!" OR we can create a truly teachable moment and model for them the appropriate communication skills we want to see them utilize.

Which do you presume is more effective? Do we want to be right or do we want communication to take place? Do we want to be right or do we want to *make it right*? In the above instance, I asked the teacher in an e-mail to come see me at her convenience the next day. When she walked in my office, instead of asking, "What in the world were you thinking at yesterday's meeting??" I simply sat down and paused (sometimes a very difficult task for those of us who are task-oriented). In that pivotal moment, she took the opportunity to speak, "I know why you asked me to come in. I thought about the negative way my comments came across yesterday and I apologize. I should have paused first to think about how my thoughts would sound out loud. I'm also trying to figure out how best I can make amends to the whole group." Wow! Even after planning my part of this conversation, I never dreamed it would turn out like this. We must give the opportunity to process to teachers if we want them to make changes in their own communication with others.

Gandhi said that we must be the change we want to see in the world. I couldn't agree more.

Mediate Parent/Teacher Conferences

What better opportunity to role model the kind of communication skills we want to have with our teachers than to ask to sit in on parent/teacher conferences? Even though it might seem like a burden of time, we need to be always ready, willing, and able to attend conferences, especially if the teacher anticipates difficulty or tension with a parent. Sometimes having that one objective person in the meeting (and that would hopefully be you) can help smooth out rough edges and encourage everyone to be on their best behavior.

A few years ago, a teacher asked me to attend a conference with her and the parents. She was worried that, after some past experiences, the parents might become confrontational. Of course I was happy to do so, but I told the teacher to be sure to let the parents know that I would be attending to answer any questions they might have. I wanted to make sure that the parents didn't feel like we "school folks" were ganging up on them. This is a necessary step because parents do feel ganged up on sometimes. In honestly and openly asking parents what they fear most about having multiple attendees at parent/teacher conferences, the response sometimes comes out, "I'm afraid you'll just take the teacher's side." How can this be, we ask ourselves, when teachers are sometimes afraid we'll do the same

Point to Ponder What problem solving approach do you use when mediating conferences between parents and teachers or even between teachers and teachers?

with the parent's side? It is a thin balance beam upon which we walk when we mediate to ensure the trust of both parties. The role in mediation, therefore, is not to pass judgment on either teacher or parent but instead to set the stage for an effective dialogue between them and reflect back what each party says.

A simple problem-solving process works well in this case:

1. Identify the problem.
2. Brainstorm solutions (no evaluation at this point).
3. Choose a solution that works best for all parties.
4. Agree to try the solution and come back together to evaluate its effectiveness.

A counseling professor in graduate school passed along some very sound advice about facilitating and mediating. "Trust the process," he said, "and step out of the way the best you can." Why is it so hard for us to "trust the process" as instructional leaders? Look at us—we have budgets to balance, positions for which to interview and hire, discipline to deal with, facilities to maintain. This job forces us to take the reins, sometimes seven days a week (faulty air conditioners and deaths in families know no difference between weekdays and weekends). "Trust the process!" we cry out. "You must be kidding!!" But trust it we must if we are to build and maintain relationships with our teachers and parents and ultimately model what we want our teachers to do.

Here are some tips to mediating that can be very effective:

◆ *Pre-conference, as necessary, with each party to assess their willingness to come to an agreement.* No good can come from meeting with parties who have clearly stated an unwillingness to work out a situation. A little pre-planning never hurts.

- *Lay some norms or ground rules right up front.* If we say out loud, "We're going to hear from Parent then we'll let Teacher speak, then we'll find some commonalities between the perspectives," then we all know what to do next and what to look for.
- *TRUST THE PROCESS.* Allow the healing to happen without jumping in every moment.

Honesty Is the Best Policy

Who hasn't experienced the frustrations that result from not being totally honest with people? Swallowing our thoughts, concerns and expectations proves a counter-productive approach as our frustration only rears its ugly head in less fruitful ways. We have all experienced times when people with whom we have worked or lived have acted in ways that invoked a sense of anger in us. Are we always honest? Not likely. Have we ever been passive-aggressive, acting on the surface as if we are unfazed, all the while searching for underhanded ways to "get even"? This is a very dangerous feeling for a school leader or administrator.

When I was the school counselor, I tried to put little cards or treats in staff boxes at holiday times. On Valentine's Day, one year, I put little boxes of chocolates in everyone's mailboxes. Within an hour, I found one back in my own box. Trying to determine who might be missing theirs, I looked at the empty boxes. Only one box was missing a treat, so I put the chocolate back in the empty box of the staff member. Two hours later, it was back in my mailbox. Curious, I approached the staff member who seemed to be repeatedly returning my small gift. "Bridget, did you get the chocolate I put in your box?" I asked. "Yes, but I don't want it," she curtly replied. "Can I ask why?" I pushed. Red in the face, she responded, "You were rude to me yesterday." *What*?! I wanted to cry out. You would put candy back in my box because you are *mad* at me . . . for something I don't even know I did???? Sometimes, a pause is just the thing we need to keep us from saying something we will regret forever. "I'm sorry, please tell me how I was rude,"

I said instead. "When you were giving a tour to parents yesterday," she explained angrily, "you passed right by me and didn't introduce me to them." I certainly remembered giving parents a somewhat rushed tour of our school, but I had absolutely no recollection of disregarding this teacher. Instead of confronting me with a simple I-message of "I was disappointed that you didn't have time to introduce the visitors to me yesterday," she instead chose to "punish" me by putting my gift back in my mailbox. Asking her about it in an open, transparent way helped clear the air.

Last year, a teacher got up and left a faculty meeting still in progress because the "duty time" had ended. I had heard the union was pushing people to do just what the contract told them to do, nothing more and nothing less. When the next week found her asking me if I minded if she left about 30 minutes early for a doctor's appointment after school, I came dangerously close to saying, "You can certainly leave but you will need to sign out and take sick time for the 30 minutes." How petty we can become if we don't keep open, honest communication in the forefront of our minds. Instead, I took a deep breath and said, "Of course you may leave early. I understand the need for doctor's appointments. I am also going to ask you for the willingness to understand when we don't finish a faculty meeting at the time your duty period ends." You know the people who count minutes until they can leave. You also know the people who don't cut you any slack for making mistakes. Most teachers are not like this, but when they are, it can be extremely frustrating. One principal I know tells his staff, "You don't want to push me on what the contract says because if I follow the contract to the letter of the law, you will lose." What are we saying about good communication and our own integrity if we fight fire with fire? Honesty wins out every time, even if it doesn't always feel like it will.

Last year brought to the surface a learning experience in honesty like no other. An issue arose in our school that caused great controversy among several people. In an issue that required a vote, a few people did not like the result. Although a vast majority voted one way, a small group of teachers were frustrated and dissatisfied with the outcome. Even after our

Point to Ponder How honest are you when your teachers complain about not getting their entire planning period one day? How honest are you when your teachers ask for you to solve a problem which you think they are perfectly capable of solving themselves? Think about a time you responded to a teacher with passive-aggressiveness, retaliation, resentment, or sarcasm out of simple frustration. How could you better respond in the future?

School Advisory Council had verified and given its approval, a few teachers remained disgruntled. None of them approached me to tell me their intention but I heard "through the grapevine" that they were planning to file a grievance about this perceived injustice. I had a choice: I could sit and wait for the grievance to be filed and then deal with the backlash that would certainly ensue (a vote was a vote and the majority had ruled; I shouldn't have to address anything, right?) or I could tackle the issue head-on.

I called a meeting of all faculty and staff the next morning and told them a story I had heard on the morning news. The story's message was one of a group of newscasters and camera crew folks who had attempted to climb Mt. Kilimanjaro together only to be thwarted by blizzard conditions. Though some wanted to continue the climb, others felt it was better to come down to ensure everyone's safety. Whatever they did, they had to make a decision quickly. The storm was rapidly approaching. (Boy, could I relate to that!) In the story, the group gathered together and made the difficult decision to end their hike and to do so as a cohesive group. They concluded that sticking together was more important than the gain of glory for a few individuals. I told this story as an obvious analogy to my staff. Then I continued, "I know a few of you here are frustrated by the vote. But I implore you to consider the ramifications of grieving something the entire school voted on and approved. We may not always agree, but we are nothing if we don't stick together." Tears were shed, my own included, and the end result was that the grievance was not filed. Did everyone walk away singing "Kum-ba-ya"? Not hardly. There were likely still a few hurt feelings. Just

Point to Ponder Conflict is never easy. When faced with a situation that needs conflict resolution, how do you deal with it? Do you run and hide, go in with guns loaded, or pull the elephant out from underneath the rug and talk about it?

as a few of the die-hard Kilimanjaro hikers might have been terribly frustrated by not reaching their individual goals, I suspect a couple of teachers were similarly disappointed in the outcome of this scenario. However, for the good of the group, we moved forward and headed down the mountain together. We healed, slowly, over time, but the lesson remained steadfast for me. Be honest and be upfront in tackling controversy.

As the superintendent who hired me told me a few weeks into my principalship, "When you are faced with a controversy, get it out there, get it all out there, and don't let anything remain hidden." Transparency, he said, was the key to any potential conflict such as this. Transparency means letting every see the real you all the time, not just some of the time. Transparency also means not engaging in behind-the-scenes meetings that entertain issues in secret that should be discussed in public. For example, do we come to a solution to a problem in a faculty meeting, then allow one or two teachers to come to us to complain about the outcome? Not if we want to maintain our integrity.

People have often said to me, "You deal with conflict so well, but I don't like conflict. I'm not good at it." Good grief!! Who *likes* conflict? Personally, I can't stand it. I do, however, choose to deal with it versus sticking my head in the sand and pretending it doesn't exist. Honesty during conflicts is difficult at best, but which would I rather deal with: a leaky pipe that needs to be repaired or a long-neglected pipe that has just burst, spilling water everywhere? For me, I choose the former.

9

When to Use and Avoid Online Communication

Long gone are the days of letters to one another on parchment paper written with beautiful quill pens. One of my favorite musicals is "Phantom of the Opera," but I have to laugh thinking of how a phantom in contemporary times would never write notes to residents at the opera house. He would simply text them or shoot them a quick e-mail. I started taking classes towards my doctorate last year and, after not having taken classes in a university setting since 1996, I was completely amazed and overwhelmed at the amount of technology that is available through the institutes of higher learning these days. I even wrote a paper on online tools for communication in public schools. The point of the literature review was to examine new technologies that make our life simpler. The caution, of course, is that using these amazing technological tools can become so impersonal.

We are so blessed to have such innovative tools at our fingertips to enhance the learning of our students, to ease the way in which teachers can access student data online, to provide yet another option for home/school contact via email, and of course to waste less paper at schools as we write more memos via email versus hard copies that must be placed in teacher mailboxes.

E-mail is a powerful tool but not one to be taken lightly.

Accepting Online Lesson Plans—Why and How?

When teachers turn in lesson plans, I like to make comments on them, ask them questions about how they planned certain lessons, and give them back to the teachers to read and think

Point to Ponder How do you check on teachers' lesson plans? How do you let them know you have read them?

about. Teachers at our school either turn in their lesson plans via e-mail or they give me a hard copy to write on and give back to them. A few years ago, one of the teachers got frustrated with the amount of paper we seemed to waste by printing out lesson plans each week. She suggested that each week, teachers submit them to me online. I have stickers set up with various notes typed on them: ones about giving students feedback, how to ask higher-order questions, how to incorporate routines and procedures more effectively in the first weeks of school, etc. I peel off the stickers and put them on the ones that are turned in to me in hard copy form. I copy and paste the information onto the ones that are submitted to me electronically.

Here is an example of one of the lesson plan notes. Please feel free to adapt and use as you see fit.

How are you increasing the level of higher-order questions in your lessons?

As you ask a basic question, consider how you could turn this question into one that requires higher-order thinking. I'll be watching for this in your lessons and in my walkthroughs this week.

Use of Wikis and Google Docs for Teacher Sharing

Another great networking tool we have found great success with is public spaces in which teachers can talk. I've done a bit of reading about Wikis and their use with students as young as elementary school kids. I also noted how well they could be used in collaboration between teachers. I thought I would do an experiment. For a couple of weeks, I did not require teachers to turn in lesson plans to me. Instead, I asked teachers to get signed on to the Wiki and participate in a discussion thread about *how* they plan their lessons. Some folks ended up being a bit frustrated by the time it took them to sign on to the Wiki. However, once they began talking to each other, it was great to see them interact about a subject that was near and dear to them. The main point was to make the Wiki not just "one more thing" teachers were required to participate in. My best suggestion, therefore, is to ask teachers to do it instead of turning in lesson plans for the week. Change is difficult, and while some teachers will jump on the bandwagon to try out a new idea, others will resist saying, "This is too newfangled for me. I'm not interested." The best way I have seen change occur with folks who resist change is to have the teachers who are using the technology successfully share their success stories in a faculty meeting or have a sharing session in their room to "show off" their new tool, product, or idea.

Years ago, we began a professional development practice that we called "Thinking Thursdays." The premise was to share best classroom practices between teachers who previously had done more of the traditional "Shut your door and teach." Primary teachers and intermediate teachers sometimes met together and sometimes met separately, but the idea was to share new and innovative teaching strategies. Mrs. Burk would announce that she would host a "Thinking Thursday" session in her classroom. It was important to meet in the teacher's own classroom to ensure that all participants had the opportunity to see all the ideas that were displayed in the room (sort of a fringe benefit to the original Thinking Thursday idea). Mrs. Burk would have snacks (maybe the most important feature, if the truth is told) and materials all laid out. It is important to note that the school set aside some money for food and items the teacher needed to support this endeavor. In this day and time of budget constraints, that is not always an easy task but one that pays off in dividends as teachers who are fed and given new resources are happy teachers. As an example, the lesson Mrs. Burk did was one on Venn diagrams. Robert Marzano notes that "comparing and contrasting" is one of the highly effective strategies that teachers should always be using in the classroom, no matter the subject matter. Mrs. Burk bought enough hula-hoops for every teacher to have two each. She described in depth how she had used these hula hoops to show a huge Venn diagram and how kids could each hold one and then "merge" together.

The sharing the teachers gained through these Thinking Thursday events was immeasurable. They began e-mailing each other after these events, saying things like, "Jenny, when we were talking about the Venn Diagrams, you said you had used something similar for your Kinder kids. Can you tell us more about that?" Harry Wong (2009) always says teachers should, "Steal, steal, steal from one another." Teachers need to get out of the mindset that they are an island unto themselves, and technology tools and social networking sites aid in that process.

Many school districts have also implemented the use of systems like Connect-Ed that are such great forms of communication for outreach to parents, but also to staff at school. When our air conditioning unit kept going out, I used Connect-Ed to relay to teachers whether they should dress for pre-planning activities prepared for a normal day or whether they should dress in shorts and tank tops. The only prerequisite to a form of communication such as this is making sure that all phone numbers are up-to-date.

Tips for Answering Emails

Just as a small child who has touched a hot stove can tell you forever and ever not to touch that stove when it's on, many administrators likely have experience in what to do and what not to do regarding e-mail communication.

E-mail has eased the burden on printing out hard copies of memos and notes that we used to send home and to the teachers. Inherent in that ease, however, comes the fact that e-mail is so very quick and easy, we can make mistakes in pressing the "send" button before we have taken the time to check our work.

Tips:

- ◆ Read the e-mail you have received to make sure you understand what the person is saying or asking. This is

Point to Ponder For example, if you read the following e-mail quickly and you miss one word, what could happen?

For the meeting that is scheduled at 3:00 on Wednesday, September 14, I will not be able to attend. Please send me the notes for it and I will be prepared.

a perfect time to "seek first to understand." One word difference could alter the understanding completely.

What tends to happen to most of us is that we are so busy (imagine that!) we either write to try to catch up with how fast our brains are throwing out ideas, or the same thing happens when we read an e-mail. We are trying to read an e-mail so quickly, we miss a word here and there that could be crucial to the message.

As an e-mail sender, then, the key might be to reiterate what you have said to ensure understanding on the part of the receiver.

◆ Put your mind in motion before putting your mouth (or fingers, in this case) in gear. When we receive an e-mail that gets up our dander, our first human reaction (after the face begins to redden or the heart starts beating more rapidly) is one of "fight or flight." The problem, of course, is that once we put the "fight" in writing and press that "send" button, there is no do-over option. So, it is imperative to begin with the end in mind and think through what we really want to say before we fire off that response to a teacher who has just written an e-mail saying something like, "If someone doesn't remove this child from my classroom today, I am going to file a grievance."

So, what should we do during this time? If all you're doing is stewing about what the other person said, that think time is not particularly productive. Instead, we need to channel the thought process towards formulating an effective way of responding. Perhaps you even want to write down some of your

Point to Ponder How would you respond to the previous e-mail?

thoughts. Just stay away from that "send" button. A teacher I know got an e-mail from a parent complaining that the teacher had called a "backpack" by a different word (book bag) and the teacher's first response was to fire back an e-mail that said, "Seriously, lady, you have WAY too much time on your hands." Likely, all of us have felt that way before, thinking we need to set this insane person straight. But the problem in responding in kind is that we lose integrity and professionalism. It may seem fun to take a shot over the bow, but in the end, we are simply building up and fortifying our wall of defense instead of breaking down the barriers to good communication.

◆ Go ahead, put your thoughts into written words, but no, no, no—still don't hit that "send" button. As you write, think about eliminating all sarcasm, condescension, backbiting or any other counter-productive communication device that might further block communication. Let's try an example.

A teacher has just written you an e-mail asking if she can leave early, again, and have someone watch her class for her.

Which might you use as a response to her?
a. "Seriously? You need to leave early again?"
b. "Good luck finding someone to cover for you again."
c. "No."

Hopefully, you know that all of the above might be what you want to say, but will likely lead to barrier-building and confrontation.

What might you say instead? Try one of these on for size or compose your own.
a. "If you can get someone to cover for you this time, go ahead. Otherwise, just fill out a leave form."

    b. "Is something going on that we can help you with?"

    c. "Let's talk when you have a minute about some options."

What you really want to do is get your point across while avoiding those barriers that keep you from building and maintaining a positive work relationship. One principal I know never sends out a potentially controversial e-mail without first having someone check it over for her. She wants to ensure that someone has looked over her words to avoid any potential hazards.

◆ Go back and read it to make sure it is what you really want to say. Keep in mind what the expected response might be from the recipient. Does the e-mail convey what you want it to say? I use this as a rule of thumb. I try never to send out an e-mail to all of my staff to make a point to one or two people. For example, if one of your teachers is perpetually late for the student take-in time in the morning, what are you trying to prove by sending out an e-mail telling the entire faculty and staff to be on time? In addition, we have to be so careful to realize that even though we know what we are trying to say or ask, not everyone will. For example, I try to use thought-provoking, sometimes rhetorical, questions to get my teachers to think about their lesson planning. Therefore, in response to their lesson plans, I might ask, "Why did you group your children like this?" A few years ago, one teacher came in my office and shut the door and began crying. She mistook my "Why" questions for questioning her motive, when what I was really trying to do was get her to think about her own thinking. I didn't realize that my "Why" questions could sound so accusatory.

While you're reading to make sure it says what you want it to say, also be sure to attach any attachments you want to include and also check for spelling, grammar, or date errors. Teachers are quite forgiving, but if we want student grammar and spelling to matter, and we want our teachers to be good role-models for that, then shouldn't administrators do the same and be the ultimate role-models? I once worked at a school where the teachers giggled behind the principal's back. They took red pens and corrected his spelling and grammar, put in commas where he had missed them, and placed correctly misplaced modifiers.

◆ Are you ready? Are you sure you're ready? Then go ahead and press "send."

Danger, Will Robinson!

While e-mail is one of the most amazing technological advances known to man, there is a huge danger in it. Remember that once something is put in an e-mail and the "send" button is pressed, there is no taking it back. You might be able to explain, "That's not exactly what I meant" if someone asks why you wrote what you wrote, but there is not a do-over button. The e-mail will always and forever be "out there" for the receiver to see, and not only to see, but also to share with others. Several years ago, we had an issue in our cafeteria that needed to be repaired. Not wanting to make it a huge deal among the parents in the community, our maintenance folks came to our faculty and staff, talked to them about it and reassured them that all was fine and getting fixed. Later that day, I sent an e-mail asking teachers to let us know if they had any questions, but asking them not to make any bigger deal out of it than it really was. The next day, a reporter from the local newspaper called me and asked if I had told my teachers they weren't allowed to talk about the issue. Taking my e-mail out of context definitely made me look like we were trying to hide something. Again, I could try to explain, "That's not what I meant," but being isolated from the rest of the email made the request sound bad.

A teacher asked me a few years ago, "Why do we always have to be professional even when the parents are so ugly to us?" My answer is, "What good does it do to get ugly right back?" It truly might feel good for about a half a second, but if we are professionals, we are required to remain professional. Crazy people are going to say crazy things, but we don't have to get crazy with them. A song by the group Point of Grace is called "Anyway." The premise of the song is that we can say something nice to a person and they might respond in an ugly manner. We say it anyway. We remain the professional because it is the right thing to do.

In e-mail messages or in-person communication, what is your point in making a statement? If it truly is to get your point across, just remember that your point only gets relayed if the message is received by the receiver. If the message is sent in an unprofessional or sarcastic way, it is likely that the receiver will dismiss it as unimportant or not worth acknowledging. Doesn't that defeat the purpose of sending the message in the first place?

So, we need to begin with the end in mind. If my goal is to say "no" to the teacher who e-mails me about wanting new materials in her classroom, what good does it do to say something sarcastic like, "You have got to be kidding me if you think we have any money for things like that right now. Hello? Have you heard we have a budget crisis?" While you may think it, what good does that do the teacher? She will likely just get riled up reading something like that. Instead, a comment like, "I know how important those materials are to you. That is why I am going to put it on a 'wish list' and when the budget improves, we can look at purchasing that." Wow, what a difference that makes, right? The teacher still might not get her materials, but at least she will likely feel like you have sincerely listened to her concern and request.

10

The Legacy of Effective Communication

Teachers Are Watching Us All the Time . . .

A second-grade teacher friend of mine was recently commenting that she has to keep some of her little girls on track when she is walking around the room teaching and circulating. "Why? Are they that distracted?" I asked. "Yes," she answered with a chuckle, "apparently by me!" It seems that one of her little girls stopped her in mid-circulation and asked, "Did you get those sandals from that new store in town?" What was even funnier, I thought, is that the teacher caught herself starting to answer, "Actually, no, a friend of mine made these for . . . WAIT! Stop! You need to listen and I need to teach." The point is that children notice everything about their teachers and our teachers are the same way about us. After an all-day meeting with my teachers, I was missing a book. One of my teachers aptly pointed out, "It should be on the table where Sara and Steve were sitting, because you had it with you when you were sitting with them but you didn't have it when you were standing up talking afterwards." Wow! I couldn't have told you half of that information, but she could because she was watching me. And apparently, I need a "keeper" because I can't keep track of my things or myself nearly as well as the teachers can do for me.

Point to Ponder Take a minute before reading this chapter to imagine what your teachers say about you when they talk to teachers from other schools. What would you like them to say about you?

Principals should realize that we are constantly in role-modeling mode, whether we like it or not. Danny Wuerffel, former Heismann winner and NFL quarterback, once spoke to a student leadership group in our county. When I asked him what he thought about being a role-model for young people, he commented that he didn't ask to be in that position. He may not have asked for it, but it is the nature of the beast when you are in the limelight of sports, media, or even the principalship of an elementary school that people will be watching you all the time. What we say, how we act, and particularly how we react are being watched and critiqued at all times.

So, if the teachers are watching us, what are they seeing? Do you talk one way and act another way? When I was a guidance counselor at a middle school, I used to teach drug education lessons to the 6th, 7th, and 8th graders. I would tell them the definition of a drug, how alcohol can harm the organs in our body, and how much alcohol a person can drink before being "impaired." I would then leave school on Friday afternoon with friends and go to Happy Hour. I couldn't wait! I looked forward to it all week. One day, I woke up thinking, "What happens to my integrity if I drink then drive and one of my kids were to see me?" "Worse yet," I thought with horror, "what if I hit one of them or one of their family members?" I totally changed my life that day. I'm not saying, by any means, that you have to stop drinking if you teach school because you are a role-model, but I am saying that integrity, by definition, is not just about talking the talk and giving great speeches. It is walking the walk and living a life of which we can be proud.

What Did You Learn From Your Teachers?

I think it is an educational truth that almost every teacher had a teacher who taught them life lessons as they were growing up. Some teachers, when asked, will tell you that the people that taught them the most were teachers of non-example—what not to do. I had one student teaching experience with a third-grade teacher who actually pulled children by the ear when she

Point to Ponder Who is one of those legacy-givers to you? What did he/she teach you? Have you ever told them what they taught you? Put down this book right this minute and take a minute to write him/her a letter of thanks.

wanted to get their attention. Yep, you heard me right. Pulled them by their *ear*! I can assure you that in all my years of teaching experience, I have not used ear-pulling as a form of behavior modification or discipline techniques. I learned from her what *not* to do.

Other people in our lives have taught us lessons that have carried us through the toughest times in our career.

My legacy giver was Claudia Edgerton, my fifth grade teacher. In 1975, my parents had recently gotten a divorce and I was living in San Antonio. I am certain that Mrs. Edgerton taught me well in the content areas of math, science, reading, and social studies. But those are not the things I remember the most. The thing I remember most from that 5th grade year was how every weekend, she would ask me about how things were going with living with my mom, but visiting my dad. She really cared. And it showed.

What Are You Teaching?

What am I teaching teachers at my school? Because I am—teaching them something, that is. I just hope that it is something that I intend to teach them. But how do I know? One of the challenges our superintendent issued to each principal three years ago was to give our teachers a survey to find out what they thought about us. "Really?!" we all wanted to cry out. Do we *really* want to know what the teachers think about us? Why would we want to do that? "Well, if you don't ask, how do you know how you're doing?" Yikes!!! So, we set out to do a 360 assessment. The questions asked about communication, discipline, leadership, support, etc. Enter the truth of human nature—even though much of the resulting survey information is positive, one or two negative comments can make some of us obsess for hours, days, weeks, even months. The negative sticks out like a sore thumb and it hurts like one, too. But, once again, principals should keep the perspective that one comment should carry just that much weight. Two or more similar comments are starting to form a pattern, perhaps a pattern that deserves at least a bit of credence and attention.

The Calm in the Storm

There is a saying that goes, "If not you, then who? If not now, then when?" If someone in the organization needs to be the voice of reason, what better person than the administrator? Sometimes, we might want to stomp and scream and kick and question, "Why me? Why do I have to deal with this?" but I figure we better do this in the privacy of our own homes. After all, someone either appointed or hired us, believing we have what it takes to do the job.

One of Stephen Covey's seven habits is to "sharpen the saw." I like to think that for me, this means that I need to have all the tools in my toolkit at the ready position. This includes the tools I need for my emotional, physical, spiritual, and professional well-being. For the professional end of it, what do I need? I need to make sure I have the support systems like a listening ear from my husband, other principals I can bounce ideas off of, good literature based on solid research and common sense about what has worked for other people, and last but certainly not least, a strong sense of humor.

I did a review of literature in graduate school on resilience. I studied what made some people more resilient than others. Not surprisingly, children tend to be more resilient than adults. Perhaps it is because we have more baggage than the little ones do. That baggage, as time goes on, weighs us down even more and becomes more difficult to just pick up and go. Overall, the literature shows that resilience is fortified by two main things: one other person to whom you can go to and vent who will always be there for you (not necessarily a parent or relative) and . . . drum roll please . . . a strong sense of humor. Apparently, that ability to laugh at one's own foibles keeps us from taking ourselves and others too seriously. As the instructional leader at my school, I believe I am charged to remind the faculty and staff to do the same. Therefore, I hope that they appreciate the funny little quips I send them via e-mail (make sure they are appropriate!) and the movie clips I use to enhance my presentations to them (i.e. one from "Land of the Lost" in which the ape-like creature is trying to explain that the big, bad guys are coming, but Will Ferrell et. al. are misunderstanding him and think he is saying "Chorizo Tacos"—silly fun, but we all laughed at how we misunderstand so much of what is said).

The point is, no matter what school district you are in, no matter whether we have budget crises or not, things are going to come up that test our mettle. The challenge for us, therefore, is to bring all our skill sets together and role-model effectively for the others, "We will weather this storm." Our pom-poms may get tattered at times, but we are the head cheerleaders and cheer we must. Besides, if not us, then who will do it?

Begin With the End in Mind

What do you want people to say at your retirement? What do they say about you now? Stephen Covey (1989) challenges people in his book on highly effective people to imagine what would be said about them at their funerals. If a co-worker were doing your eulogy, what would they say? Well, let's take it just a few steps further. Imagine that all the names of your faculty and staff are put into a hat and one name will be drawn to speak at your retirement. No matter what name is drawn, do you know what they would say about you? At the end of your career, what will people say about your ability to be straightforward and shoot straight from the hip? What will they say about your honesty and integrity? What will they say about your ability to communicate and motivate? Whatever you wish they would say at the end of your career, you had better practice and work toward each and every day. Good communication and relationship building cannot simply be done every second Tuesday of the month. It has to be interwoven into the very fiber of our beings each and every day. If I want those great things said about me at the *end* of my career, I need to walk the walk each and every hour and every day.

Be Right or Make It Right? What Is Your Main Mission?

If I want to role-model good communication for teachers, I should likely ask myself that important question about what my main goal is in each encounter. I try (and try, and try, and try) to remember to ask myself what my motive is: do I want to be right or do I really want to make this situation right? In a disagreement with a teacher about a grading policy, do I wind up demonstrating a combative stance when they disagree with me (or more likely, with the policy) or do I role-model what I want them to do, which is be solution-minded, focusing on the end result versus the problem? The point is if I want the teachers to be open for brainstorming, I had better do and role-model the same.

Keep It Child-Centered

If I am ever in doubt about the proper way to solve a problem, whether it is one with a teacher or a parent, the running header flashing in my mind at all times should be, "Keep in mind what is best for the child and you can't go wrong." That is the legacy that has been left to me by my former assistant superintendent, who told me my first week on the job that I could *not* go wrong if I kept this in mind. I might be unpopular, I might make some people mad by not doing what they wanted me to do, but I will not ultimately go wrong as I keep the best interests of the child or children in mind when making a final call.

The Emotional Bank Account

The emotional bank account we build with each and every teacher in our school is the ultimate legacy we leave behind. Can they trust us to do the right thing? Can they trust us to be honest with them? Notice I'm not saying, "Will they do the thing that will be popular?" While it isn't loads of fun to do or say something that will be unpopular, sometimes that is what we have to do. That is why emotional bank accounts are so crucial, for all the employees at our schools, not just the people we really love. Principals need to work hard to build them up so they are there in times of need for withdrawal. A great relationship will not be ruined by a recommendation to re-think a parent/teacher issue as long as there is enough "emotional clout" there in the first place. We all know who we can say certain things to and who we have to walk on eggshells around. The eggshell people are those who we are about at overdrawn status with and we need to find the overdraft protection required to keep the relationship from falling apart completely.

We Are Teachers. What Are We Teaching?

No matter what we are doing, we *are* teaching each and every day. The question is one of what we are teaching. We teach both implicitly (through modeling, leading faculty meetings, parent/teacher conferences, etc.) and explicitly (through actual professional development sessions specifically geared toward communication, relationship building, and parent/teacher conferencing).

At the end of our career or at the end of our lives, someone may stand up and speak for us. The music teacher who we all cheered for during pre-planning about being cancer free died a few months later. While I was tremendously honored and enormously humbled to be asked to speak on our school's behalf about her, it was important to choose just the right stories. I mentioned that she and I had sung a duet together just a few months before—a song from the musical *Wicked* called "For Good." The words in the chorus say, "Who can say if I've been changed for the better? But because I knew you, I have been changed for good."

I believe we are all changed by each person we meet. The question is: what do they say about us after we have moved? Retired? Passed away? What do we want them to say? Whatever we want them to say we did or said or were, those are the things we must do, say, or be today and every day.

Bibliography

Cash, R. (1993). *The book of positive quotations* (2nd ed.) (S. Deger & L. A. Gibson, Eds.). Minneapolis, MN: Fairview Press.

Covey, S. (1989). *The 7 habits of highly effective people.* New York: Simon & Schuster.

Lemov, D. (2010). *Teach like a champion: 49 techniques that put students on the path to college.* San Francisco, CA: Jossey-Bass.

Lerner, H. (1985). The dance of anger: *A woman's guide to changing the patterns of intimate relationships.* New York: Harper & Row.

Marzano, R., Pickering, D., & Pollock, J. (2001). *Classroom Instruction That Works.* Alexandria, VA: Association of Supervision and Curriculum Development (ASCD).

Maxwell, J. (2009). *Ifferisms: An anthology of aphorisms that begin with the word if* (Grothe, M., Ed.). New York: HarperCollins.

Pausch, R. (2008). *The last lecture.* New York: Hyperion.

Roosevelt, E. (1960). *You learn by living: Eleven keys for a more fulfilling life.* Louisville, KY: Westminster John Knox Press.

Wicked. (2003). Schwartz, S.

Tingley, S. C. (2006). *How to handle difficult parents: A teacher's survival guide.* Fort Collins, CO: Cottonwood Press.

Underwood, C., DioGuardi, K., Fredericksen, M., & Laird, L. (2010). Undo it. On *Play On* [CD]. Arista Nashville.

Wong, H. K. & Wong, R. T. (2009). *The first days of school: How to be an effective teacher.* Mountain View, CA: Harry K. Wong Publications, Inc.